D1092384

Compassionate S .... &
Empowerment

A Conversational Guide

Unbreakable Woman

Maura Barclay

Preview Edition

Library of Congress Cataloging-in-Publication Data
Barclay, Maura
Unbreakable Woman
The Art of Compassionate Self Defense

ISBN-13: 978-1484099698
Confidence 2.   Empower Yourself 3. Demystify Criminals
4. Skills 5. Test Knowledge

Dedication:

This book is dedicated to all of my tribeswomen
in LA, Denver and Seattle. They have inspired
me with their power, strength
and healthy femininity.

Also to the wonderful men in my life who
have demonstrated remarkable nurturing,
support and healthy masculinity.

I am grateful to all of these wonderful people
for providing the love,
patience and guidance to
help me walk this path.

NAMASTE

Table of Contents

INTRODUCTION

*1 out of 5 women has been the victim of an attempted
or completed rape in her life time.[1]*

If you're one of the "1's", the following words may have
crossed your mind along your healing journey: "I never
thought it would happen to me."

If you're one of the fortunate four, you might be thinking: "I
hope that never happens to me."

Unbreakable Woman® was created to help you rewrite your
story, to take control of the situation, to get yourself out of
danger or avoid it altogether. By the end of this book, you
will be able to say:

"I have the power to fight and escape.

I have the intuition to avoid and prevent.

I have the awareness to stop being afraid."

There is no secret weapon to hide in your purse, or secret
move to practice in the gym. The secret to becoming an
Unbreakable Woman is compassion. Listen with compassion
to the women who came before you so we can learn from
their stories. Understand that we are not slayers hunting an
army of monsters; we are women who are dealing with

---

[1] Center for Disease Control - 2010 Violence Prevention Survey: http://
www.cdc.gov/ViolencePrevention/pdf/NISVS_Report2010-a.pdf

damaged men. An example of this was courageously donated by a friend of mine. (some of the details have been changed for her safety)

I wish I would have had one of your seminars when I was in my early 20's. I was raped when I was 21 on Spring break by a VERY LARGE football player that was into body building. I had no idea what to do. It was something I NEVER thought would happen to me, especially with so many people partying around me. I used to be unable to talk about it, but now I find it therapeutic and I am debating becoming an advocate.

I was too scared to go through all the court stuff and the prosecutor told me he couldn't guarantee any type of conviction, so we ended up plea bargaining. My attacker went away to prison. It was a guarantee of a punishment, and I didn't have to relive all the details in front of a bunch of people. I still have fears that someday he will come after me for putting him away."

My friend's story was my call to action. I want to help change the refrain from "I never thought it would happen to me" to "I have the power to fight and escape" and ultimately, "My intuition told me he was trouble so I avoided him like the plague." Unbreakable Woman is not a therapeutic recovery book. This book is about keeping you safe through awareness, prevention and empowerment.

I wrote this book for every woman who wants to live a more empowered life. It's designed to shift your thinking from victim to survivor, to transform fear into confidence and provide realistic tools to help you right now.

There are true stories, donated by friends and colleagues, throughout this book. I hope they serve as touchstones for your own empowerment and help those who have suffered a crime to heal and move forward.

If you are reading this book, you are taking the time to familiarize yourself with a subject that most avoid because it's so scary. The act of educating yourself is a big step toward eliminating the panic that comes from not having any idea who you're dealing with or what to do. Your confidence can be significantly increased just by unmasking the villain and learning about where this type of man comes from, how he operates and how you can avoid or escape a confrontation with him.

Unbreakable Woman is meant to re-introduce you to the effective self defense skills you were born with. Skills that you may not even be aware are in your arsenal, but are there waiting to serve you anytime, anywhere.

By the final pages of this book, you will understand how much power and control you have in common self defense scenarios and beyond.

Although an actual confrontation will always be scary, you will have a clear role in your own rescue. That alone may be able to pierce through a panic response and keep you connected to your intuition.

The creation of Unbreakable Woman came from my own path of healing the wounds of a tumultuous childhood. A childhood that left me feeling victimized and angry as an adult. Through intensive training in martial arts and Yoga, I was able to see that the only way to truly heal was to find forgiveness for my own mistakes and faults first. Once I forgave myself, I was able to better understand my parents and see them for who they are: just people.

In my case, I am grateful that their misguided parenting was mild, compared to what some children suffer through. The moment I found compassion for my parents, I stopped blaming them. When I stopped blaming them and took responsibility for myself, I stopped being a victim. My fears evaporated and I quickly became an ardent advocate for myself.

The compassion in "compassionate self defense" comes from finding forgiveness for ourselves first, forgiving those who have trespassed against us and understanding the motivations for those who would seek to do us harm. Compassion is our ultimate strength and a source of incorruptible power.

The path to our greatest personal power is paved with forgiveness and compassion.

Take good care yourself. When you take care of you, it benefits girls and women everywhere.

Thank you.

SECTION I: Confidence Becomes You

"We can't solve problems by using the same kind of thinking we used when we created them." - Albert Einstein

HOW THIS BOOK WILL HELP YOU

☞ See How Confidence Is The Ultimate Weapon

☞ Understand How Self-Defense Classes Work

☞ Transition From Fear to Confidence

This book started out as a one-page handout at my seminars. I noticed that there was a lot of note taking at my presentations and I kept getting requests for more information that attendees could take home with them. Eventually, the handout evolved into the pages you are about to read.

Since I like to learn in a linear, systemized way, I organized this content as a seminar I would have loved to have taken back when I was 20 and scared to walk across campus after dark.

The chapters in this section will help you understand the connection between education, fear reduction and increased confidence. It will show how compassion is empowering, help you distinguish between "good" and "bad" fear and outline some common scenarios where danger can quickly escalate.

This book is designed to build your confidence by unraveling the victimization process through the following steps:

1. Scenarios - We'll discuss common situations that can become dangerous. You'll learn how to recognize the red flags of criminal manipulation and how you can successfully navigate to safety or avoid them altogether.

2. Mindset - We'll examine how your attitudes and mental habits may be unintentionally generating fear, creating disempowerment and putting you at risk. You'll discover a more empowering way to perceive, process and talk about this subject.

3. Decoding The Criminal - We'll take a closer look at general categories of criminals, uncover their manipulation tools and better understand where their behavior comes from.

4. Your Power - You'll learn critical awareness skills and fundamental physical tools that will help you create a safety solution anytime, anywhere.

5. Scenario Recap - At the end of the book, we'll look back at the original scenarios through more educated and confident eyes. You'll see how layers of decision making or lack of awareness contributed to a situation becoming dangerous. By making a plan for each scenario, you'll

have an arsenal of action steps to take when the moment
calls.

THE PROBLEM

According to statistics released from the CDC National
Intimate Partner and Sexual Violence Survey (2010
Summary Report):

> Nearly 1 out of every 5 American women have been raped
> in their lifetime and 1 out of 2 have experienced sexual
> violence other than rape at some point in their lives. [2]

That means every two minutes, someone in the U.S. is
sexually assaulted[3]. And that's just based on what is reported.
Most likely, the incidence is more frequent than the statistics
reveal.

I want to be clear about the context for this book. If a
survivor is still struggling with the natural after effects of her
trauma, which can take years to overcome, she may not yet
be ready to contemplate these topics. Everything on these
pages is for those who are ready to grapple with all facets of
this daunting subject. When I ask the women in my seminars

---

[2]

Black, M.C., Basile, K.C., Breiding, M.J., Smith, S.G., Walters, M.L., Merrick, M.T., Chen, J., & Stevens, M.R. (2011). The National Intimate Partner and Sexual Violence Survey (NISVS): 2010 Summary Report. Atlanta, GA: National Center for Injury Prevention and Control, Centers for Disease Control and Prevention, pgs. 18, 19

[3] Rape Abuse & Incest National Network: http://www.rainn.org/
statistics

about their readiness to deal with the things they fear the most, there are three consistent themes I keep hearing:

1. "I'm not strong enough to defend myself." So untrue. Women do not appreciate how much power they posses both mentally and physically and how little it actually takes to injure a much larger opponent. (See Section IV, *Welcome To Your Physical Skills*)
2. "I don't know martial arts." Self defense doesn't begin with physical skills, it ends with them. Personal safety is the result of many subtle but potent skills that are at work long before anyone gets close enough to actually put hands on you. (See Section IV, *Six Critical Skills*)
3. "I think I would freeze if I ever met one of those monsters!" When women de-humanize criminals by calling them "monsters", it only gives the criminals more power to intimidate and dominate. Introducing you to the mortal man behind the monster is a big part of fear reduction. (See Section III *The Straw That Broke The Camel's Brain*)

This book will take take you on a journey from fear to empowerment and give you tools that you can use everyday to maintain your safety and advocate for yourself in any situation.

EDUCATION

In many ways, personal safety and empowerment for women boils down to one thing:

Confidence.

There are many ways to increase confidence and reduce fear around the threat of violence. Education is the key to the kingdom. Acquiring physical skills is a great way to feel more confident, but you need to spend time learning them and they must be maintained. Increasing your understanding about how criminals think, where they come from, the many self defense options available to you right now for successful avoidance and escape can effectively help increase your confidence as quickly as you are reading this.

When it comes to your personal safety, confidence is a weapon that is always sharp and you don't have to dig it out of your purse.

My first Compassionate Self Defense seminars featured a mix of physical self defense and play. I was afraid that no one would show up if it was just a lecture. Plus, the initial seminars were in Equinox fitness clubs in Los Angeles so there was an expectation that the class would have a physical component.

I always knew that physical skills weren't a part of the Unbreakable Woman program, but I didn't know if women would appreciate the value of the information itself. Particularly since self defense classes traditionally emphasize physical skill building.

Here's my issue: It's unreasonable to think that the millions of girls, teens and women who all need self defense information will be able to attend a live physical skills class or ongoing martial arts training. This is our current paradigm for women's safety and empowerment and quite frankly, it stinks. It stinks because it's limiting. What about the millions who don't have access to classes or aren't comfortable in that environment?

SELF DEFENSE AMERICAN STYLE

I believe our culture's approach to women's safety is back-asswards. If you're trying to figure out how to make something float, you can't focus on the sinking problem. When it comes to self defense, there are some areas where we're missing the boat.

By emphasizing the need for women to learn how to fight like a man, we're presuming that the problem is that we're physically weaker and lack the combat skills of our would-be opponents.

Ergo, if women just knew how to fight, we could defend ourselves and these dangerous people would no longer be a threat. It would be wonderful if it were that simple, but lack of physical fighting skills and proportional strength is not the problem at all. We're focusing on the physical inequalities between men and women as if that is the problem. That's not the problem. The problem is there are emotionally damaged boys and men walking the streets looking to take someone's power. They want an easy mark.

As I got older, I realized that being safe was much less about being able to whip out a devastating reverse hook kick and much more about two critical elements:

1. Awareness
2. *Visible* willingness to stand up for yourself

Then it dawned on me.

> **Information is the great mind changer.**
> **It can shift your mind from a state of**
> **fear to confidence.**

To test this theory, I began every seminar with five questions. The answers from the women and teens attending were remarkably consistent. The following is a word-for-word recounting from my seminars:

Q: What are women hoping to learn at a self defense workshop or class?
A: Protection. Self defense skills.

Q: What kind of self defense skills?
A: Physical skills.

Q: Why are we compelled to go to a self defense workshop or class?

A: Fear of being attacked. Because we are afraid. News reports.

Q: What do you come away with after the self defense work shop?
A: Confidence. Less fear. Paradigm shift.

It was the 'paradigm shift' that lit me up like Hugh Hefner's birthday cake. The physical classes also educate women about the victimization process, how the attacker thinks and gives physical solutions that give women the feeling of being safer. Women also get something very important: Experiencing the surprising strength and power their bodies are capable of.

Physical self defense classes teach you how to control your role in a confrontation. The confidence comes from understanding and believing in your power.

For women who have never been very physical in their lives, it's incredibly emboldening to feel the power of their punches, kicks and elbows. Although skills learned in weekend workshops often get rusty without practice, the confidence remains. That is the golden ticket to safety.

Once women have become awakened to their power, criminals want nothing to do with them.

Classes and/or workshops can provide a fundamental change in their attitudes about a scary subject that leads to an increase in confidence and a reduction of fear. A winning combination that will help keep them off of criminal radars.

The final question:
Q: Is it necessary to go through physical training to get this confidence or change of attitude?
A: No.

Much to my surprise, all of the attendees quickly agreed.

Once illuminated, the light bulb is on forever.

Believe it or not, you already possess the physical strength you need to defend yourself. At the end of this book, there are fourteen true stories of ordinary girls and women, with no special training, successfully defending themselves. That said, I highly recommend getting into a physical self defense class like IMPACT. If for no other reason than to prove to yourself that you CAN DEFEND yourself and you are PLENTY STRONG. Plus, throwing punches and kicks is incredibly liberating -- and it's good exercise! We need more outlets for our natural, healthy anger.

THE POWER OF COMPASSION

Although violence against women has been emotionally devastating our gender since the beginning of time, it has only come into the national spotlight as a legitimate issue in the past 40 years. The subject was ushered into the public consciousness in 1976 with the establishment of the National Center for the Prevention and Control of Rape. In 1994, Congress passed the Violence Against Women Act (VAWA) and the created the Office on Violence Against Women as part of the U.S. Department of Justice.[4]

Rape is a very grim topic that usually causes wincing and a desire to change the conversation. Unfortunately, our puritanical society still has us associating sex with rape when it's about power and violence. A survivor of physical abuse may feel pride in overcoming her ordeal whereas a rape survivor is culturally conditioned to feel shame, as if she was ruined somehow. This inhibits women from talking about it and generates a lot of fear and anger.

Although anger and fear are completely natural and legitimate responses to violence against women, they don't help us deal with the problem. Compassion, on the other hand, is a positive-*proactive* strategy that can create a tremendous amount of inner strength and personal power.

---

[4] Practical Aspects of Rape Investigation: A Multiple Disciplinary Approach, 3rd ed., Robert Hazelwood, Ann Burgess

WHY COMPASSION

- When we find compassion and forgiveness for ourselves first, for anything that has happened in the past then forgive those who trespassed against us, we can heal, let go, move on and prevent history from repeating itself.
- Compassion can help us see the humanity in dangerous people which can make them seem less scary. The less we fear, the more likely we are to keep our heads about us.
- We are stronger when we utilize our natural inclination to be compassionate so we can more effectively empower ourselves.
- Compassion means we yell, scream, hit, kick or bite a criminal who is threatening our life because we love and protect ourselves, not because we hate the criminal. We are much more likely to come to our own rescue when we act out of love and protection, like we would for a child in danger.

Compassion does NOT EXCUSE NOR CONDONE any form of violence against women. It reduces fear and gives you a more powerful place to deal with these criminals.

Unbreakable Woman is different because it's *compassionate* self defense.

Fear and insecurity can attract power-hungry people. Anger, although it can be a good deterrent for violent criminals, can eat you alive. Compassion is an incorruptible power that can help you defend yourself and empower you in all aspects of your life.

Humans as a species have a long and unfortunate track record of fearing what we do not understand. Once we have a modicum of knowledge about things we fear, it takes the spooky out of it and allows us to consciously manage any fear we may still have.

Understanding can take us from irrational to rational; ignorance to tolerance; fear to confidence.

Consider a brutal serial rapist who targets high school girls and leaves them in a ditch to be discovered by passing hikers. An unrelenting, intelligent sociopath who is portrayed by the media as an unstoppable, major league monster. When I think of monster, I think super-natural beast and demonic powers. The personification of evil itself. A soulless, dark creature trolling quiet communities with a roll of duct tape, latex gloves and over-size trash bags in his trunk. These crimes are so hideous and far removed from my reality, I can't process the kind of animal that commits them. It's overwhelming. I can't imagine defending myself against such a monster. Can you?

Now, what if this same criminal were portrayed by the media as a person who was born into bad circumstances, suffered from severe physical abuse and neglect as a little boy, actually witnessed his drug abusing mother's murder at the hands of a violent boyfriend, wound up a troubled teen and had a long history of drug abuse and prison? It's easier to wrap your mind around the "how" a person could come to commit such crimes. We've lifted the veil to see a broken, tormented human being.

Compassion helps us deal with the criminal and the "why" behind their crime. There is no "senseless violence". If you ask the criminal, their actions made perfect sense to them.

Finding compassion for the young boy who suffered a great deal means understanding the circumstances that could produce these kinds of people. His adult behavior was a result of torment forged in the flames of childhood neglect and violence. This allows you to transform the monster into a mortal man. Even the most sick, twisted, scary and dangerous man, is still just a man. Can you defend yourself against a man? Yes.

Having compassion will ultimately help you. Understanding the young boy who never had a chance is a much more powerful place to be, rather than fearing the dangerous adult he has become. It's not to feel sorry for him, it's to help you see how much control you have when faced with the dangerous adult. When you apply the skills you're about to learn in this book, you will be more evenly matched than you could imagine. How much control do you think you would have against a monster? Wouldn't you have to be a monster too? Unbreakable Woman is about you cultivating all the natural skills you already have and being who you already are.

NO JUDGING

Even as you are reading this, "bad people" are out there. They're doing things. They're up to stuff. If you spend your time judging them, labeling them, you are creating a wall of separation between them and you that's not real. The more you judge, the thicker the wall. When you're out and about and relying on that wall to protect you from a dangerous person, you may be unpleasantly surprised. If you are hanging on to your right to judge criminals, I ask you: What does it accomplish? Do you feel safer or do you just feel better about yourself? Stay out of judgement and be present in the world of all things are possible.

If you need reassurance that you are a good person, get it from the the good things you do, not the bad things you don't do.

The line that separates us from criminals is thinner than you think. We are all capable of committing violent acts given the right circumstances. Imagine if you saw someone in the midst of brutally beating your elderly parent or molesting your 3 year-old child. Would you hesitate to intervene physically? How far would you take it? I submit that a person might "see red" and find themselves standing above a corpse with no recollection of what happened. Are you a monster now?

When it comes to reducing your fear of dangerous people, the most powerful attitude you can adopt is, "There but by the grace of God go I."

The sooner you accept that each of us has the same shadowy dark side as every criminal in the history of human kind, the less afraid of "them" you will become. They have untapped goodness in them just as you have untapped darkness in you. Being a "good" person is a choice we make moment by moment. It's work and not everyone can handle it. When circumstances change, so can our perspective and moral compass.

YOUR STRENGTH

In many ways, women are built much stronger than men. Men who truly understand women get this. Our strengths are not obvious. Our true power doesn't come from biceps and braun. Men who don't understand women or are deeply threatened by our innate fortitude refer to us as the fairer sex. Although very difficult to master, our greatest strengths sprout from our natural inclination to nurture and eventually lead us to the three most potent powers in all of humanity: forgiveness, healing and compassion. Anyone who has had to genuinely practice these can tell you how difficult they are and how much internal strength is needed to walk this very, high road. If you know women who have walked the path of true forgiveness and compassion, I'll bet you can see their power from a mile away. Make no mistake, they are peaceful warriors.

⚠ TRUE STORY

This was sent to me by a courageous woman who found my Unbreakable Woman page on Facebook. She is a perfect example of a woman who has walked the difficult, high road. She is actively working to stop the cycle of violence.

I was raped in 1987 and began working with victims of sexual violence in 1998. In 2007, I took a job where I would also be working with perpetrators and their families. I was scared to death about who I would meet and how I would handle it. A wonderfully compassionate counselor with whom I had worked reminded me of exactly what you said. She said, "They are only people. People with their own problems. And many of them have been victims themselves."

FEAR ALL MEN?

Within every human being are the ingredients of a dangerous killer. Each of us has the potential to kill another person. At the end of the day, the only difference is ability and will to make choices and choose the right action.

How can you know if the new person you just met has an interest in harming you or another person? If your intuition hasn't weighed in, only time and observation of their actions will tell. Trusting people is part of a fulfilling life and asking people to earn your trust is self-esteem lesson number one. People who have cultivated their desire to hurt others are looking for trusting or fearful targets.

The majority of men are good people, choosing "right action", living their lives with a moral compass that points true north. They are our husbands, fathers, brothers, uncles, friends and male colleagues. I have wonderful and supportive men in my life who I am thankful for. In fact, one of the most incredible books I've read about women's self defense was written by Gavin DeBecker, a remarkable man who has dedicated his life to the safety of others. Let's not forget the countless male police officers, investigators, lawyers and judges who make it their business to protect the rights women and work tirelessly to see that their abusers or murderers receive justice.

On the other hand, there are men whose sensational crimes make it into the evening news, who's insidious crimes go unreported and all those in between. Please remember when reading these chapters that if a particular kind of criminal makes your blood boil as it does mine, it's the behavior we rage against, not the gender or the person.

There are plenty of cases of matricide and patricide by daughters, not to mention jealous women abusing and brutally killing other women and men. Although it's easy to get myopic about the male "monsters" who rape girls and women, always remember that sociopaths can be any gender, ethnicity, socio-economic class and sexual orientation.

TWO KINDS OF FEAR

With all this talk of conquering fear, it's important to recognize that not all fear is bad. In fact, it can be a life saving survival impulse.

THE BAD FEAR

Unhealthy fear incites panic, overwhelms you and eventually leads you to check out mentally. It could be neurotic, like a phobia, which can be extremely difficult to overcome and may require some professional therapy to resolve. Needless to say, phobias can severely impair your ability to think, get present and help yourself.

Panicky fear can come from either a lack of awareness or denial. When distraction prevents awareness, it's easy to get surprised and subsequently overwhelmed. With denial, by the time you acknowledge the danger it's too late.

THE GOOD FEAR

Healthy fear sprouts from your intuition and it lets you know you are in the presence of a dangerous person or situation. Be prepared: With this healthy fear you may get an enormous dose of adrenaline that will make taking action challenging.

PRACTICE SCENARIOS

In martial arts studios across America, a self defense class usually starts like this:

"It's 3:00 AM, you're trapped in a dark alley by a guy with a knife..."

This really drives me bananas. Given, it's a situation worthy of discussion, but why do we always accept the scenario and never stop to ask, "Excuse me, how in the name of Pete did I wind up in a dark alley at that hour?!"

That said, hypothetical scenarios can teach us a lot. Although every situation is unique, there are some common threads that you can follow. Studying scenarios can help you build confidence in your ability to recognize a problem when you see it. Also, being able to put yourself in the scenario and mentally practice successfully avoiding or escaping harm is a crucial skill called *Mental Training* (see Section IV).

These scenarios will allow you to practice:
1. Seeing where the lack of awareness leaves someone more vulnerable to harm.
2. Seeing red flags that are generally consistent throughout each type of situation.
3. Trusting yourself so when you receive intuitive information and notice these red flags, you can act without hesitation.

Each scenario is deconstructed at the end of this book to allow you to see how the lessons we learn can be applied as aware, empowered women.

1. <u>STRANGER DANGER</u> - The quintessential self defense situation where you feel threatened by someone you've never seen before. Although this is at the heart of what women fear the most, stranger-to-stranger violence is statistically the least likely violence you'll encounter.

a- Work place parking garage/lot

b- Mall or grocery store parking lot while putting things in the car

c- Walking or jogging through paths that are somewhat secluded

d- Getting lost in an unfamiliar city

e- Repair/delivery men and contractors

2. <u>ACQUAINTANCE DANGER</u> - Someone who is familiar to you who has gained your trust to some degree. This accounts for more than 80% of all reported assault cases. This is where women need to focus more of their attention.

a- Co-workers

b- Neighbors

c- Casual dates and boyfriends

d- Friends of the family

3. <u>ABUSIVE RELATIONSHIPS</u> - A relationship that most likely started out very good, but then rapidly devolved into dysfunction and danger.

IN DETAIL: STRANGER DANGER

These scenarios are either based upon actual events or have come from concerns and fears brought up in my seminars.

The Parking lot of your work place - Leah arrived at work on time but the garage was jammed. She had to park where there was space available and the spot wasn't very close to the elevator. Up against some deadlines, she works a little late and is one of the last people to leave. Upon arriving in garage, she notices a man loitering. Unsettled, she turns and walks toward her car. Luckily, her car is in the opposite direction. She feels like she needs to look over her shoulder but she doesn't want to appear nervous like she is watching him. She picks up the pace, hearing only the echoey clip-clop sound of her heels as she walks. Leah keeps thinking one thought: *get to the car.* As she arrives at her car safely, Leah reaches into her purse to get her keys, feeling relieved and a little silly. As she disarms the alarm and opens the door, she is suddenly shoved hard from behind...

Mall or grocery store parking lot- In the middle of the afternoon Donna is walking to her car with a cart overflowing with grocery bags, dog food, 24 packs of water etc.
This is just the first of many errands she needs to run and she is behind schedule. She realizes she will be late to pick up her kids from their play date so she calls to let the parents

know. She pops the trunk and starts to put bags in when, a man appears abruptly, surprising her. "Oh, I'm sorry" he says. "My goodness, I didn't mean to scare you."

She catches her breath and despite still feeling uneasy, she tells him it's fine. "Let me help you with those," he offers. "No thank you. I can manage," she replies. "Well, aren't you the model of a modern women," he says, "Please, I insist. Happy to lend a hand to a damsel in distress." Although a little put off by his creepy comments, she doesn't want to get into it with him so she continues putting bags in the trunk, leaning in to keep them organized since there are so many to load, "That's okay. I'm in a rush."

He looks at her disapprovingly and says, "It doesn't make you less independent if you let someone help you." He notices the family stickers on her rear window, depicting a man, woman, two girls, a boy and a dog. "I'll bet your kids keep you jumping." He laughs a little and looks at his watch. "I'll bet it's just about time to pick someone up from school. C'mon, four hands are quicker than two, let's get you on your way." She considers the heavier items in her cart and reluctantly agrees. She pulls her keys from her purse and unlocks all of the doors. Instantly, his expression changes and he lunges at her...

Walking or jogging through a somewhat secluded path - Beth is an avid outdoor jogger and loves to explore new places. She downloaded some great new music, charged up her iPod, drove to a new path, and after a few warm up stretches, she begins her route. It's beautiful weather and the path is in bloom with flowers, buzzing bees and dense green leaves on all the trees. Her favorite song comes on so she pumps up the volume. She notices a man on a bench just off the trail. Although he is lying down, his eyes are open and he's not sleeping. He's dressed a little warm for the weather and looks like he just came off a construction site. This seems strange to her but it's a nice day to relax outside so she doesn't think much about it.

As she heads down a narrow section of the path, surrounded on either side by dense forest, she becomes aware of another runner behind her and judging from the closing distance, they are trying to get past. She glances over her shoulder to motion for them to pass and she notices that the runner is wearing jeans, work boots and a sweat shirt. This "runner" suddenly lurches forward, wraps his arms around her, and tackles her to the ground...

Getting lost in an unfamiliar city - It's starting to get dark as Lori searches for the great new bar her friends texted her about 30 minutes ago. They are already two drinks into happy hour and want her to join them. Using the address in the text, her GPS led her to an unfamiliar part of town. Her friends raved about the cheap, signature cocktails so it would make sense that it was a hole in the wall in a sketchy area. The only parking space close to the address appears to be an abandoned parking lot so she gets out and walks around looking for the bar. She walks for a good five minutes, seeing only run down apartment buildings and a few store fronts.

Lori can't find the bar or the address. Finally, it dawns on her that her friends must have gotten the address wrong and she is in a bad neighborhood. She starts to get nervous and quickly turns tail to head back to her car. While walking, she tries to call her friends but her battery is out of juice.

A wave of panic comes over her. She passes a busy laundromat when she notices a couple of guys are walking toward her on her side the sidewalk. She knows they are trouble. She hugs her purse tightly to her side, looks down and walks as quickly as she can, hoping they will ignore her. As she approaches them, one of them steps in front of her and says, "Hey, do you have a cigarette?", she stops and says no. He says, "How about some change. You got any change?" as his friend walks around and steps behind her...

Repair men, delivery men and contractors - Nicole is showering when the water turns ice cold. Covered in goosebumps, she towels up and heads to the basement. After monkeying with her hot water heater which is probably from the Kennedy administration, she knows she has to call a repair professional. She can't afford to replace it so she goes online searching for a company promising the cheapest, quickest service. After deciding on a company that boasts "local contractors at your door in minutes!", she makes the call and gets dressed.

As advertised, there's a knock on the door 20 minutes later. Hair still wet, she answers. A burly, late 30-something repair man dressed in sloppy "work blues" with a paint splattered tool box that looks older than the water heater, waits to be invited in. He looks Nicole up and down and says, "You like you were just in a hot shower." Repair man humor? Maybe, but it instantly creeps her out. She hesitates for a moment. He definitely gives her the willies, but she doesn't want to seem rude. "I can't fix the problem from here." he says, not joking. She takes an instant disliking to him, but figures it's more important that he be better at fixing faucets than making conversation. Nicole leads him straight to the basement. After she answers a few basic questions and he starts to work, he looks her up and down again. "Your husband is a lucky man." Uncomfortable and feeling the need to appear confident, she says she's not married but has a boyfriend. "Well, he's got his hands full with you, I can tell ya that. Why don't you go get him so I can explain the problem with this." She smiles weakly, says he's out with friends. Feeling unsettled, she excuses herself and says she'll be back down in a few minutes.

Upstairs in the bathroom, she is drying her hair. She bends down to put the dryer away and when she looks in the mirror, she sees him standing behind her. Startled, she spins around to face him, heart beating out of her chest. "Oops. Didn't mean to sneak up on you like that." She regains her composure. Not wanting to appear afraid, she casually asks, "Are you through already? Can you show me what you did?" Nicole tries to leave the bathroom, but he stands at the door, blocking her...

IN DETAIL: ACQUAINTANCE DANGER

Co-workers - Jessica has been working with Mike for about seven months. They get along and work well on projects. Lately, he's been teasing about asking her out. It was cute at first, but it's become a little annoying. She has no desire to have a workplace romance with him or anyone else, but wants to prevent any awkward tension between them. So every time he "jokes" about it, she always laughs and redirects him gently.

Finally, he actually does invite her out for an after work drink. He seems like a nice enough guy, other people seem to like him and it could reinforce their teamwork dynamic. Plus, colleagues often socialize after work so she decides to go. Mike shows up in her office a couple of hours before they're supposed to leave and offers to drive, adding that it would be easy to drop her at her car afterwards. Always looking for ways to reduce her carbon footprint, she agrees. At the bar, the waitress serves them both a couple of rounds and Jessica is really enjoying a lively conversation. Then, Mike makes a blatant sexual advance. She very gently and politely declines. It's getting late and she hints that she's ready to go but he wants to hang out a little longer. He says, "Just one more drink. C'mon, it's the least you could do after shooting me down." he adds playfully. Despite his levity, a wave of anxiety passes over her, but she doesn't want to cause tension at work tomorrow, so she agrees. Suddenly impatient, he goes to bar for the last round of drinks.

Jessica wakes up in her car, disoriented, dizzy and nauseous at 4:37am...

Neighbors - Leslie has seen Bill outside a few times. They have waved at each other but never spoke. He keeps to himself but seems friendly enough. His house is well kept, he drives a nice car, has a 9-5 job and he's married with kids. It's a mild, sunny weekday and Leslie is cleaning the house when there's a knock at the door. She opens the door to find Bill standing there. She notices that he is clean shaven, dressed in a crisp white shirt and jeans. He says that he's home sick from work and doing a little laundry to surprise his wife, since she's always doing so much for him, but he ran out of detergent. He asks to borrow enough just for one load so he can finish and apologizes for any inconvenience.

It occurs to her that he doesn't look unwell, but it is a reasonable request and an opportunity to help out a neighbor. "Of course. I'll get it for you." She goes to fetch the detergent when he quickly follows her in. She notices he doesn't wait to be invited in, but lets it go. How could she ask a sick neighbor to wait at the door? She directs him to the couch to wait. As soon as he walks in she has an odd thought. All of a sudden, she realizes that she is alone in the house with him. She shrugs it off and goes to get the detergent.

She arrives moments later with the whole bottle to find him gone. "Bill?" No answer. Leslie looks around and finds him around the corner in an adjoining hallway, admiring family photos. "Look at those kids. You must be a very loving mom." He says. "Thanks." She says, a little puzzled. "Here's your detergent." She tries to hand him the bottle but he asks again for just enough for one load, apologizes for the inconvenience and promises to get out of her hair. So she goes into the kitchen to put a tupperware container together for him when she hears his footsteps behind her...

Boyfriends (or dates) - Jackie and Scott have been dating for a few months. She's not sure if he's the one, but she really likes him. He's cute, has a decent job and the sex is great. A few things she has noticed though, Scott is a big drinker and has gotten drunk to the point of passing out on numerous weekends. Also, he's a kinda mean to waitresses and his friends are total jerks. When he's around them, he turns into a complete tool. But nobody's perfect, right? She figures it's so hard to find a cute guy with a decent job, sometimes you just have to put up with some stuff you don't like.

After a party at his friends house, he drops Jackie at her place. She's a little tweaked because he got pretty hammered and insisted, to the point of being obnoxious, that he was "fine to drive...now get in the car!" He wants to come in but she wants to call it a night. It's a Thursday, she has to be up early and quite frankly, she is exhausted having just spent the last four hours tolerating the constant misogynic banter from his punk-ass friends. He says "Pleaaaase...? Just for five minutes then I'll leave. I promise" and gives her the puppy face. With a heavy sigh, she caves. She says, "Okay, but just for five minutes". He asks for a beer but she will only give him water or coffee. He doesn't want it. He plops down onto her couch, patting the cushion next to his, inviting her to sit. He's still pretty buzzed and Jackie is sober so she is not finding this cute at all. Yawning, to give him a not so subtle hint, she joins him and tells him she really has to go to bed. She doesn't want to be a bitch, but he's becoming super annoying. He promises he will leave after she gives him a good night kiss.

The kiss turns into making out, but she has already made the mental decision to not go any further. Jackie stops, pushing gently into his chest saying softly that she needs to get up early. He interrupts her by kissing her more passionately. She can tell that he's getting aroused so she pulls away and asks him to go. Undeterred, he playfully lies on top of her, saying he promises to go after a good night lay. She tries to push him off, telling him to leave. In a flash, his demeanor turns from playful to angry. He puts his weight into her, pinning her down, gathering her wrists over her head, squeezing tightly and yells in her face that she is a prick tease...

Friends of the family - Alissa is the only girl of four kids. Mr. Bergen and his wife are good friends of her parents. They have been friends for years. When she was a toddler, Mr. Bergen loved to play with her. He would often pop in to visit with her parents, with and without his wife, and Alissa would inevitably end up in his lap. As she matured, she would catch him staring at her. When she did, he wouldn't break his gaze, instead he would continue and smile at her. This made her uncomfortable because he's an adult; so she shyly looked away, hoping he would stop noticing her this way.

When she entered her pre-teen years, if ever Mr. Bergen and Alissa were alone in the same room during parties or BBQ's, he would never miss an opportunity to get behind her, massage her shoulders, tell her how pretty she was and how lucky her boyfriend must be. His touch didn't feel right but she didn't want to make him mad by saying no. She felt guilty for not liking this affection. Upon leaving, he would reach his arms out and say, "Can your favorite uncle get a hug goodbye?" If she shyly refused he would playfully charge at her, sweeping her up in his arms, to everyone's delight. This made her a little uncomfortable but she didn't want to upset her family.

He would write her personal notes in beautiful greeting cards, telling her about the challenges in his life and how his wife isn't a good listener. His cards included gifts, each one more expensive than the last: $10 iTunes gift card, $20 Amazon card, iPod Shuffle. He would never mail them. After a visit, they would appear in Alissa's bedroom, like magic, and always ended with instructions not to tell anyone so her brothers wouldn't find out and get jealous.

She feels totally weird now because he makes her uncomfortable but she enjoys being showered with so much attention. He would strike up chats via email, which would sometimes include instructions to turn the ringer off on her phone so he could call her when she was in bed and not wake anyone up. When she turned 13, he invited her to go to the mall with his wife to pick out a birthday gift. His wife had a last minute work schedule conflict so it was just Alissa and Mr. Bergen. Her parents had no reason to object to the invitation. After all, they've all known each other for years and he's practically family...

IN DETAIL: ABUSIVE RELATIONSHIPS

Husband or Boyfriend - Ella is fresh out of college and paying her dues at a menial job she doesn't like very much. After a particularly bad day, she goes to a friend's party and meets a really hot guy. After a few dates, he seems to be everything she has ever wanted. Smart, funny, charming and has a good job. She quickly falls head over heels. They have been dating for a little more than six weeks. Since she spends almost every night at his place, he suggests she move in with him. He tells her how much he loves her, how happy she makes him and how he wants to be with her all the time. She's barely making ends meet at her lousy job and she loves him so it's perfect. Living with him is fantastic. It feels like a honeymoon.

Then, after a few weeks, Ella notices that every time she spends time with friends or family he calls and texts constantly. When she gets home, he is cold and distant which makes her feel terrible and like she's done something wrong. Ella decides that if she makes their relationship more of a priority, she can avoid that horrible cold shoulder. So she spends less time with friends/family and more time with him. This seems to make him happy. Eventually, she stops seeing her friends because it just causes too much grief.

He surprises Ella one day by suggesting that since he makes enough money, she should quit her crappy job. He has already said that he wants to eventually marry her and give her babies so, why not?

Then, after a couple of months, she notices that he seems to be hanging out with his friends more and more and staying out later. When he comes home, he's drunk and not so nice. He says that she has become boring and a nag so he has to hang out with his friends to have a little fun. After all, he is the one working long hours to make sure the bills are paid. Ella takes issue, saying that she's happy to get another job and this makes him angry. Very angry. He gets in her face and yells that she has changed and is making him miserable.

The next morning, Ella brings up the fight from the night before. She wants an apology but he tells her she's overreacting. He was just tired and had too much to drink and she is overly sensitive. The fights continue, when she tries to walk away, he blocks the door. His anger grows into rage. He blames her for all of their problems. If she makes a mistake or forgets something, like picking up his beer at the store, he screams at her, calling her stupid and worthless. The fights get worse, he grabs her by the shoulders and threatens her by saying sometimes she makes him so mad, he feels like squeezing the life out of her with his bare hands. When she tries to talk to him about these threats the next day, he acts like nothing happened. He tells her she is crazy and has a wild imagination. One night, after a particularly rabid argument, she declares that she is going to a friend's house to stay the night. He runs into the kitchen to grab a knife then chases her into the bedroom...

"If you don't like something, change it. If you can't change it, change your attitude" - *Maya Angelou*

REWIRE BAD ATTITUDES

☞ Reframe The Self Defense Scenario

☞ Discover Your Blind Spots

☞ Reclaim Control of Your Safety

SELF DEFENSE: ATTITUDE IS EVERYTHING

The chapters in this section show how some of your perceptions, mental habits, behaviors and beliefs can play an enormous role in keeping you safe (empowering you) or putting you in danger (feeding your fears).

This section is designed to show you how being powerful is not just something you reserve to use only when you're in danger. Empowerment is something you need to cultivate all the time. Advocating for yourself is a habit like anything else. When you do it consistently in your personal and professional relationships, then you are much more likely to do it when confronted with a creepy stranger.

There are many ways your beliefs and attitudes about potential threats of violence are shaped. The media, pop culture, personal experiences, stories from friends and family, even the language we use to think and talk about it, all play a part. Knowing how to physically defend yourself won't do you much good if your fear overwhelms your ability to utilize those skills. By addressing your mental and emotional landscape first, you can discover where you may have some unhelpful attitudes and reframe your ideas so they are more empowering and supportive.

No matter what has happened to you, you have an opportunity at any given moment to *change your mind* about how you want to deal with it.

That point was never more perfectly delivered than by beloved Notre Dame football coach and motivational speaker, Lou Holtz:

> **"Life is ten percent what happens to you and ninety percent how you respond to it."**

TALKING YOURSELF OUT OF YOUR POWER

Stranger Danger doesn't just apply to how you perceive others, it applies to how others perceive you.

You could have a .357 snub nose Magnum revolver in your cute purse for all they know. You could be a 3rd degree black belt in Brazilian Jiu-Jitsu! The only thing strangers know about you is what you tell them with your body language and attitude.

When it comes to you, YOU have the advantage.

Sex offenders and violent criminals are often wounded, cowardly, disempowered people looking for someone who won't put up a fight. Anyone looking for an easy take down isn't going to try their luck with someone who acts like they know how to handle themselves. How would they know if you can handle yourself? *Because you tell them with your body language and attitude.*

In the book <u>Profiling Violent Crimes. An Investigative Tool</u>[5], one of the convicted killers interviewed says he can tell by the way a woman walks, her body language and the look in her eyes if she is a good target. There you have it. Straight from the horse's mouth.

---

[5] Ronald M. Holmes, Stephen T. Holmes, Profiling Violent Crimes. An Investigative Tool (SAGE Publications, 1996, Second Edition)

POWERFUL YOU

Here are some excellent habits that can keep you safe and empower every aspect of your life:
- Be aware of your environment. ALWAYS.
- Own your circumstances and don't blame others. NO MATTER WHAT.
- Advocate for yourself. ANYTIME, ANYWHERE.
- Realize you are already possess effective defense skills and can protect yourself. PERIOD.
- Think about how you could successfully defend yourself, verbally and physically, in multiple scenarios. SEE YOUR SUCCESSFUL ESCAPE.
- Accept that damaged, dangerous people are allowed to want anything they please. They are not, however, allowed to take anything from you without your permission. PERIOD.

When you consistently practice these ways of being, you become a force to be reckoned with. No cowardly, disempowered stranger will want to tangle with you. That is the advantage of being *visibly* willing to advocate for yourself. Project that willingness for all to see.

DANGEROUS YOU

Some behaviors can actually invite danger. I call these 'target' behaviors because they are the equivalent of putting a target on your back:

- Walking through life distracted, detached, not concerned what's going on immediately around you.
- Ignoring your intuition when it says that someone is bad news.
- Constantly pointing the finger and blaming others for your circumstances.
- Giving strangers the power to influence your opinion about yourself.
- Worrying what someone might do to you.
- Denying the existence of damaged, dangerous people who will ruthlessly take advantage of anyone who will let them.

Many women may not even be aware that they are unwittingly contributing to their unwanted circumstances. For them, disempowering habits are second nature. This is a wake up call! Each of those habits is like a wedge, driving a deeper divide between you and your personal power.

If anything on the 'Dangerous You' list sounds familiar, it's important to acknowledge it and take steps to improve your habits. Beating yourself up or judging yourself will only push you further into disempowerment. If you have discovered that you are doing some of this stuff, that's *good* news.

Once you've learned about the existence of a problem, you are more than half-way to solving it.

If I accomplish anything with this book, it's to help you identify which habits may be disconnecting you from your power. Once you're aware, you can take action to protect your precious self.

DISCONNECT #1: DISTRACTION & INSECURITY

Are you happy with your body? Your job? Your clothes? One of the key ways that we allow ourselves to become disconnected from our power is when our insecurities distract us from seeing when we need to take action to avoid impending danger, whether it be in a bad relationship or with a stranger in a parking lot.

Our culture, while making progress in the fair and equitable treatment of women, also seeks to separate us from some of our most powerful aspects. Insidious media portrayals continue to infantilize, objectify and demand unnatural, unobtainable bodies while domesticating us right out of our survival instincts. It's no accident we find ourselves in need of self defense and empowerment training.

As women, we are mired in a sticky, acrid tar pit of cultural expectation. If you want validation, you had better be nice. And it's a bonus if you are pretty, large busted, confident and smart... but not too confident or smart, that's intimidating. We must balance all of the things we're supposed to be as they're piled precariously on top of our heads like an enormous Las Vegas-style headdress made out of full cups of piping hot tea. Our culture has us so busy trying to walk without spilling, it's no wonder we don't think to step out of an elevator when a creepy person gets in.

Hurry up and get married, would you? Aren't you pregnant yet? Did you get the raise? Did you get my email? Did you preheat the oven? Is that a grey hair??

Our media works around the clock to ensure that we are distracted and insecure because fearful people buy more stuff. True fact. Meanwhile, there are plenty of violent criminals who rely on our distraction and insecurity so they can exploit it.

Example: It's 10pm. Susan is waiting for her friend outside their apartment complex so she pulls out her phone and start texting, "Downstairs. Waiting." A male stranger walks by and she continues to text, not looking up but she feels him watching her as he walks by. In that brief moment, he totally creeps her out. After a few seconds, he turns around and walks back to her and tries to strike up a conversation. Her instinct is to get away from this guy, but she doesn't want him to think she's a stuck up bitch. So she reluctantly talks to him even as the hair on the back of her neck stands up.

- Distraction: Susan chose to focus on texting instead of addressing the person coming into her space. Sometimes a casual, indifferent "Hey." can communicate that you see them, you're not afraid of them and you aren't interested.
- Insecurity: Her intuition told her everything she needed to know about the situation. Her fear of

being perceived as a bitch is drove her decision making.

Another self-esteem pitfall is many girls grow up being told never to get angry. They're told it's ugly or a sin[6]. Somehow, in our culture we are only allowed to calm things down, smooth things over and be a composed peacemaker. That would be great to shoot for, but in the real world, when we're treated unfairly it's maddening. Anger is natural and can be a healthy expression of your truth, so long as it doesn't dominate your entire life.

People who are trying to manipulate, disempower or exploit you must be told in no uncertain terms that you won't tolerate it. If it takes getting angry to provide that feedback then that's what it takes. Repressing anger is very unhealthy and can lead to disease and destructive outlets such as alcohol and drug abuse. Sometimes our own anger or rage is scarier than the experience that produced it. It can get dark in there. Mix it with shame and you've got a depression cocktail that can land you in bed for months.

For many women, the wounds from the past leave an indelible mark of shame, guilt and fear on their psyche. It's time to suck out that poison before it can be allowed to motivate any more choices we make. When we're motivated

---

[6] Lois P. Frankel, <u>Women, Anger & Depression Strategies for Self-Empowerment</u>, Health Communications, Inc., 1992.

by these things, we make bad decisions. Sometimes, deadly decisions.

DISCONNECT #2: FANTASY THINKING

Do you like to walk around in rose colored glasses? Many women cope with the reality of our violent culture by creating a fantastical world view. The fantasy is simple and childlike in innocence. It's a world view where there are no dangerous, desperate people around us and we all intend good things for each other. How could peace and love be a problem? It seems harmless enough, right?

When we want the world to align with our idealized, cooperative, non-violent ways, it's an egocentric projection of our own morals; a stark denial and a lack of respect for the reality of people who are different than and/or dangerous to us.

It's dangerous to routinely expect everyone around you to think and act like you do.

When we do this, we may open ourselves up to be targeted. The desire to hang onto this innocence can lock your mind in the fantasy while an awful reality is about unfold, with you in it, whether you want to believe it or not.

It's that split second where the reality of the moment feels so scary, you become overwhelmed and opt out. You choose to train your inner gaze to what you want to see rather than what is actually happening before your eyes.

Every woman I've talked to who has experienced a physical trespass, and I poll frequently, confided knowing that something wasn't right. This is both appalling and hopeful.

Appalling: Because these women talked themselves out of their primary self defense impulse and right into a traumatizing incident.

Hopeful: Because it means intuition was working.

We must reprogram the value of AWARENESS and SELF TRUST back into our lives.

One out of five women in the US knows all about what happens when we ignore, explain away or in any other way resist intuition. When they beat down their truth so they could focus on what amounts to denial or political correctness or fantasy, bad things can happen.

A very good friend of mine shared her story about living in one of those "fantasy-realities" when she was in her 20's. She described her past as a "miserable life story". She had just graduated college. She wanted to get away from her past and start fresh in her first single apartment. To cope with the wounds of her childhood, she chose to see her new community as a kind of haven where only good, helpful people live. Bad things happened to other people who lived in other places.

⚠ TRUE STORY

"I was in my early twenties when I was raped. . . or technically 'sexually assaulted' by police definition in those days. As I think back to that day, I remember being carefree. I had no sense of fear. I had just finished a telephone conversation with my boyfriend and I was collecting my things to go and meet him.

Like I had done everyday since I moved into my quaint little single apartment, I opened the back door without a thought that anyone would be waiting there.

But that one day was different . . . I opened the door and a man in a black ski mask walked in and spun me around. My back was up against his body, his arm tightly around my chest, a sharp object jabbed into my ribs and a deep threatening voice telling me to do as he says or I will get hurt.

Still today I can only see a face covered by a ski mask . . . and I still hear the threatening voice (a low whisper in my ear) telling me not to scream . . .

He pushed me from the back door through the kitchen into the main room and then onto my futon. It is a sickening memory . . . why didn't I fight . . . I should have fought back . . . but all I remember was feeling paralyzed and my vision was blurred.

I was very comfortable in my apartment until that day. I never would have thought this would happen to me . . . As a woman – I was very insecure about myself. Moreover over I was not always "aware" of my surroundings." -SP, Los Angeles

Her need for a safe haven to cope with her past created a false sense of security. She never thought she needed to be aware. Mix that together with personal insecurity and it created an opportunity for a power-hungry coward to exploit.

DISCONNECT #3: DENIAL

I've heard denial in many forms from many different women, but there seems to be couple of common themes. Here's a classic example of denial.

This comes from a friend of mine who is very independent, smart and practices awareness of her surroundings as a rule.

⚠ TRUE STORY

My boyfriend and I had just attended a concert in a venue on the edge of a bad neighborhood in Chicago. The show ended late. Instead of taking a train home as usual, we decided to walk through the sketchy streets together to check out the historical buildings. I felt pretty safe since my boyfriend was big, tall and athletic.

As we walked, I noticed a young guy standing on the sidewalk, leaning against a fence. I noticed him because it seemed strange that he was just hanging out there, doing nothing in the middle of the night. I felt immediately that he was trouble. My instinct was to get away from him as fast as possible, but then I thought, "I don't want to live in a world where I have to be afraid walking down the street!" So we kept walking. We passed by that weird guy and nothing happened so I felt justified. Moments later, two more guys came out of the shadows and we were pistol whipped within an inch of our lives. -HK, Chicago

Her intuition came in loud and clear, she just didn't like the message. She ignored it. Instead, the voice of denial shouted down her truth and bad things happened.

If you want to live in a world where you can safely walk around at night, make safe choices and heed your intuition. It's not magic, it's how to make that world view a reality. When you see someone that your intuition clearly tells you is bad news, choose to listen to your gut and avoid that person.

Going knowingly into rough neighborhoods late at night, ignoring your instincts and expecting to be safe is like jumping into the ocean and expecting to stay dry.

If you want to live in a place where it's safe to walk down the street, you make it so. Certain neighborhoods can be dangerous at certain times. Sometimes the "safe" streets are peppered with creepy people that you must cleverly avoid. Change the things you can, accept the things you can't and be aware of your surroundings regardless.

DISCONNECT #4: POLITICAL CORRECTNESS

This story came from a Yoga friend of mine.

⚠ TRUE STORY

My friend was walking down a familiar street alone at night when she felt the need to look behind her. She glanced over her shoulder and saw a young man and said she knew instantly she was in danger. Being an intelligent and tolerant person, she also noted that he was a different ethnicity than she. Her fear of being a racist trumped her instinctive foreknowledge of impending danger. She trampled over her truth with, "I am not a racist!" She kept walking, ignoring him, until he eventually caught up with her and pounced.

This is a perfect example of how amazing intuition is. Her first survival impulse was subtle and came when her intuition told her to turn her head and look behind her. Once she turned, she got a second, more obvious message.

Generally, we try to talk ourselves out of our inner knowledge by analyzing the message against what we want to believe. Her rationale that "all black people aren't dangerous" trumped the loud and clear truth that this *person* is dangerous. The more evidence we decide to stack up against our intuition, the less likely we are to listen to our inner wisdom.

To this phenomenon I ask you: Do you want to be safe or politically correct?

When emotionally balanced 'good' people are met with the conflict between contributing to ethnic stereotypes versus our personal safety, we falter. This is a particularly corrosive problem since it's very easy to exploit.

<u>Women, Hear This:</u>
Intuition is color blind. Intuition knows when you are in danger. Intuition responds to intention of a person, not their ethnicity.

A dangerous person is a dangerous person regardless of ethnicity or socio-economic status and must be treated as such.

For the those of us who grew up in a time more tolerant to open discrimination, we're hard-wired to want to give different ethnicities a break to balance all those who didn't. I get it, but that attitude is actually racist too.

If you sincerely desire to contribute to the fair and equitable treatment of all people, then let someone's behavior influence the way you treat them. Deal with the person, not the skin. If your gut tells you that a person who is a different ethnicity than you is trouble, give yourself permission RIGHT NOW to treat that dangerous, unbalanced person like the criminal he or she is. To hell with how it looks.

On the flip side, don't assume someone is safe because you are the same race. Dangerous people come from all socio-economic and ethnic backgrounds. I've met intensely creepy people who wear $3000 suits, drive gorgeous cars and live in McMansions. The only way to know is to listen to your gut.

DISCONNECT #5: NEED TO BE LIKED

Of course we want to be liked, we're communal creatures and that's part of our female wiring. Realize that this desire can cause you to unintentionally give your power to someone who doesn't have your best interest in mind.

The power to influence you is a gift that you alone have the right to give and take away.

Practice giving this very special power only to those people you know that have earned your trust. Brace yourself: some people will not like you. That's normal and healthy. Care about what your friends and trusted allies think, not some doofus who really wants to buy you a drink.

Allowing random people to influence your opinion of yourself opens the door for manipulation.

MISTAKEN IDENTITY

As you practice listening, accepting and acting on the messages from your intuition, you may make mistakes.

Heaven forbid! Well, it's true. As you are learning to listen and discern the difference between pure intuition and irrational fear generated by cultural conditioning or phobias, you may make an incorrect judgement. Accept that possibility. You could absolutely freak out on a totally decent person. Even if this happens, forgive yourself immediately. After all, you are not out to try to make anyone feel bad, you are simply trying to live a life free from violence. The learning curve isn't always pretty, but it's a truly important life skill worthy of suffering through a few embarrassing mistakes.

Our intuitive knowledge is as close to infallible as we're going to get, but it still has to be translated through the filter of our brains.

If you make a "listening mistake" you can always apologize. A reasonable person will forgive you. Knowing this may help you pierce through the static to heed your intuition. When your personal safety is on the line, feel free to make as many mistakes as you need to.

RECONNECT TO YOUR POWER

Do you say nice things to yourself on a daily basis? Ever? Are you conscious of negative self talk when you're doing it?

More and more studies show that the emotional reactions we have, whether to people, ideas or situations, can have a direct impact on our bodies and can take a real toll. Even the very thoughts we think can create chemical reactions in our bodies that can either help us or hurt us.

One of the gifts I received from Yoga was the ability to become consciously aware when I was doing/saying/thinking something destructive. It became a powerful tool for awareness and change. Although it's a life long endeavor, you can begin with simple things to help cultivate your connection to your intuition and powerful habits.

RECONNECT #1: LIVE CONSCIOUSLY

Conscious living. It may sound like some ooky-spooky, new age mumbo jumbo, but it's actually one of the most empowering concepts I've learned.

Conscious living is simple: Accept that your *personal world* is a masterpiece created by you with all of the choices you make and have ever made. The good, the bad and the ugly. Choose not to regret a single choice. Instead, see that choice for what it was at the time. A choice, made consciously or unconsciously, that contributed to a situation which allowed you to see who you are, what you're made of and what's important to you. Own it.

Your life is the canvas, you are the artist and your choices the brushes and paint.

It is not easy. With the exception of choices made for us when we were too young to choose for ourselves, the bad, awful stuff you would rather forget was in some way a product of a choice you made. When we manifest unwanted, painful things, we tend to take our hands off the steering wheel, jump into the back seat and say, "Don't look at me, I didn't do this, I'm just a passenger!"

If you can manage to hang onto the wheel, no matter how bumpy the road you've chosen, you will never loose your control over your life.

RECONNECT #2: CULTIVATE AWARENESS

In order to make conscious choices, you have to have a degree of awareness. They feed each other. The moment you stop to consider what you are about to do, you drop into the moment, become present, aware of your environment and instantly connect to your power. All it takes to create that moment of consideration is to consciously breathe.

Your mind can transport you anywhere you want to go. When you leave the present moment, you are no longer connected to your body. Your body is always in the moment. Use your breath to drop your mind into your body, into the present and into your keen awareness. To reconnect your mind-body bond, stop what you're doing, consciously inhale into your belly and silently say, "I am breathing in..." then pull your belly in as you empty your lungs and silently say, "I am breathing out..." Practice this conscious breathing technique and soon you will be able to "drop in" after only a single breath.

When it comes to your personal safety, make smart choices by obeying your instincts. That may not seem like an earth-shattering revelation, but when you frame your reality around making smart, conscious choices, years pass and you realize you are able to go just about anywhere and do just about anything. Safely.

**Ultimately, you create your safe world.
You take care of you.**

Hungry or scared animals are dangerous, but the world isn't inherently dangerous to an aware person. There's little difference between a lion looking for it's next meal and an unbalanced human looking to feed their personal power deficit by bending someone to their will. You can go anywhere you want, but certain places are more likely to compromise your safety. If you insist on visiting those places, go with your intuition armor on and have an exit plan handy. When you go to the zoo, stay out of the lion's den.

RECONNECT #3: CHOOSE YOUR WORDS

War of words. That's how women fight. Words are our daggers, our arrows and if you get us mad enough, our heatseeking missiles. When we unleash a carefully chosen tirade, we can leave the shrapnel of our fury buried deep into the psyche of those who incurred our wrath. If you have ever been on the receiving end of a verbal slaying, you are familiar with the damage it can do.

As far as I'm concerned, it's no different than getting hit with fists except the bruising is invisible, sometimes deeper, and can take longer to heal.

It's important to recognize that our words can have immense power and we must not abuse it. Choose to use your power for good.

Women are skilled with words. We're excellent communicators. This is primarily how we relate. Analyzing how we choose our words can be key in shifting our world view.

I'll bet you don't even realize the potential power you have in the words you use. Making a shift toward carefully chosen words to think and talk about things can create new emotional and behavioral associations. Using this process, you will be able consciously choose stronger words which can result in more empowered feelings, attitudes and actions.

From now on, consider your words "power tools." Naturally, these tools will extend into your ability to compassionately advocate for yourself. The second you consciously choose what to say, you're in the moment. You are aware. You are more powerful.

Thought, words, emotions and behavior are all linked. They all feed one another. Their common bond is your body. We take in conversations exactly as we would a ham sandwich. They both come into our bodies through an orifice, get processed, metabolized and exit an orifice. The only difference between taking in information and eating lunch is which orifices they come and leave through.

On the surface, how you speak may seem unrelated to your personal safety. I assure you, they are intimately related.

Power comes from within and without. Even when you're feeling scared, choosing *Powerful Speech can give the appearance of confidence which can turn the tide of a dangerous situation in an instant. (* Section IV, Six Critical Skills)

THOUGHTS AND WORDS WORKING FOR YOU

Another power tool is to use positive words instead of negative words to express what you want. Here's a classic example of using positives versus negatives to create a desired effect: "Don't panic." versus "Stay calm." Which one of these phrases makes you feel more at ease? Always choose words and thoughts that are oriented on the outcome you want. Stay focused on where you want to go. If you always have your eyes trained on where you don't want to go, guess where you're going?

Words are powerful when there is truth and conviction behind them.

So why bother paying so much attention to what your saying?

Derek Sivers, philanthropic entrepreneur, best selling author of <u>Anything You Want</u> and frequent TED conference speaker, once said, "How you do anything is how you do everything."

Thinking and speaking like an empowered person helps you BE and empowered person.

I'm sure you've heard the expression 'fake it 'till you make it'. That completely applies here. If you can make small, doable changes every day that bring about a deeper sense of confidence and empowerment, that's the best self defense there is. It could prevent you from having to throw fists and feet to defend yourself down the road.

When you are going about instituting these changes in your life, notice if you are a big fan of words like 'try' and 'hope'. Those two words are like Twinkies of the word world.

Empty calories, zero nutrients, zero potency. 'Hope' is passive and 'try' lacks conviction. Instead of 'trying' to do something, 'work toward' or 'be in the process of' it. Get active! These small changes to the way to talk about something can affect the way you think about it and ultimately, act towards it.

In the timeless words of Yoda, "DO or DO NOT. There is no try."

A quick how-to:

1. Think about a small, attainable change you would like to make. Something really doable like 'take one conscious breath every day'
2. Stop saying "I'm trying to change"
3. Start saying "I am making simple changes every day"

Declare your intention to yourself, your friends, allies and the world. You said it, now you're committed to follow through. Just do your best.

WORDS THAT SEPARATE US FROM OUR POWER

We like words like 'try' and 'hope' because they distance us from the possibility of failure and also distance us from our power to execute. It's only natural to fear failure. But everyone fails. When you were learning to walk, did you fall down? After your first fall, did you say, "Screw it! I knew this would happen! I'm crawling from now on." Taking steps to move forward in light of the possibility of failing is *exactly* what builds confidence and courage.

Coping with failure is EASY compared to coping with the disappointment we feel when we don't even make an attempt to help ourselves.

Reserve the word 'try' for the times you're testing something out, like a new food or a car. When it comes to making changes to live a more empowered life, there is little room for trying. This is plenty of room for doing, failing then dusting yourself off and doing again.

If you're "hoping" for something that's within your control, you don't need to hope. Even when there are variables beyond your control, you can maximize the likelihood that you will get what you're after.

Here's the difference:

1. *I hope I can get an A in this class:* Do the work. Know what's expected. Talk to the teacher to refine your understanding of what's expected. You work hard, study, you fulfill all of the requirements and learn the content until it becomes second nature. You know the answers on the test. You get an A. This is within your control.

2. *I hope I get a raise:* Kick butt at your job. Show that you have earned your wage increase by demonstrating specifically how your work has produced measurable

results for your department and the company as a whole. You are confident enough to ask your team leader (better words than boss, supervisor or manager) for a raise. The decision may include factors beyond your control, but you've done everything within your control to manifest your raise.

3. *I hope I don't get attacked by that creepy guy walking toward me:* Intuition has let you know that stranger walking toward you is bad news. You cross the street and take note of what businesses are open and what people are around you. If he follows, you either duck into a public place, ask someone for help or get on your cell phone immediately and call 9-1-1. This is within your control.

It's our job to give ourselves every opportunity to see our desires fulfilled.

Choosing your words consciously may seem like a trivial pain in the butt. However, it is a crucial habit that can keep you consciously in the moment, aware and connected to your immense personal power. For the sake of yourself and the world, take your power with you everywhere you go. Whether you're seeking change in a relationship, at work or within yourself, use positive powerful language and consciously choose words that will move you compassionately and confidently forward. Every change, however small, absolutely counts!

STOP USING THESE WORDS

This chapter is devoted to transforming how you perceive the whole process of victimization by changing a few key words you use to think and talk about it. Certain words trigger emotional reactions which are translated through your behavior, like body language. Here's a quick example:

RAPE

How do you feel since you took in that word? Rape. When we vehemently *don't* want something, we tend to shrink back, away from it. We get smaller, in avoidance. Do you feel that happening in you? Maybe even in a small way? How about this word:

FIERCE

How does that word make you feel? Do you see how we associate ourselves with the words and process them in relationship to ourselves? When we want something, we get bigger, more assertive. Making ourselves more visible to the desired object or outcome.

Words matter.

When criminals are looking for targets, your body language speaks volumes about your state of mind. Many women report "going into shock" when physically threatened and being unable to defend themselves. The shock they refer to is being overwhelmed by fear and panic. If particular words illicit a fear from you, it's time to take back your power. Replace those words with others that inspire a more healthy or empowered emotional reaction.

FOUR BAD WORDS THAT STEAL YOUR POWER

Here are some words that cause us to emotionally run amuck.

BAD WORD: ATTACK

How does seeing that word make you feel? Are you having an empowering experience?

Does your body language change when you hear that word? When I ask this question in my seminars, all of the women shrink back, their shoulders draw in to make themselves smaller. Notice what happens in your body and any images that come to your mind when you digest this word.

ATTACK.

Is your body transforming into a shape or posture of confidence? Based on the reaction of my participants, this word sucks. I don't like it and I refuse to use it. 'Attack' is a victim's word.

The word 'attack' implies that someone is active (initiating) and someone is passive (receiving). Since women aren't doing the majority stranger attacks, which role do we automatically assume for ourselves?

A lion attacks a gazelle, a shark attacks a tuna, predators attack prey. We're not gazelle, tuna or prey.

Screw this word. This word is dead to me.

BETTER WORD: FIGHT

How does it feel to process this word? What's happening with your body language?

What images come to mind? When I give the word 'fight' to the women in my seminars, they lean forward, shoulders broadening and chins up. It is amazing to watch the instant change in body language. 'Fight' appears to be something more familiar, less scary and while not desirable, a fight is doable.

Even though attendees still felt scared, daunted, unsure, it was a whole different array of emotional responses which translated into much more confident body language.

We've all been in a fight. Most likely verbal since that's our M.O. From here on out in this book, any interaction that comes to conflict, whether verbal or physical, will be called a fight.

Because that is what it is sisters. A fight to preserve your right to live without violence. It's ludicrous to me that anyone would have to fight for a life free from violence, but it's a reality of our species. The sooner you accept this, the less likely you'll ever have to do it.

BAD WORD: PREDATOR

What pops into your head here? Is it helpful?

Does it promote confidence? Doubtful. Here's the feedback I've been getting about the lovely word 'predator': Creepy. Scary person. Scheming killer.

It doesn't take a rocket scientist to see that this word also needs to go in the trash. This is another one of the most non-helpful, massively disempowering words associated with this topic that breeds fear. No one knows what to do with predators. They are "inhuman monsters". Possibly with supernatural powers for all we know.

Again, it implies that all the power and control is in the hands of only one person. The person with the knowledge and a sneaky plan.

The word denotes a cunning, homicidal willingness to to stalk someone through the night wearing night vision goggles, ready to pounce on an innocent unknowing victim. No. No way. Screw this word too.

BETTER WORD: OPPONENT

How does that make you feel? Can you handle it? What images come into your head?

I like this word, 'opponent', because it vividly creates the imagery of two equally matched people. *Two people.* And you'll see in the stories of successful dealings with these opponents in later chapters that they can be more easily defeated than you thought. Just because your opponent may come to the table with a few advantages, such as physical strength and a sociopathic desire to hurt people, you are also an opponent who comes to the table with a share of advantages.

One critical advantage that may ensure your escape: Your opponent has underestimated you.

BAD WORD: VICTIM

This is a slippery slope. Conceptually, it means that you were involved in something against your will. When we are faced with survival situations beyond our reality or imagination, we use the word victim. We need this word for legal purposes and to describe people who met their end in a natural disaster, plane crash, accident, etc. Fine. That makes sense to me. When used to describe the living, it's a nasty, steaming pile of bad idea.

The word victim says "powerless".

When it comes to empowerment and self defense, I believe this word is THE most disempowering and corrosive for our psyche. It's like a thick, stinky slime that sociopaths can smell a mile away.

Don't let anyone slap that victim label on you, no matter what. Victims are prey. They are statistics. Reserve the word victim for describing a person or people who didn't survive their ordeal.

BETTER WORD: SURVIVOR

Being a survivor means you went through something and LIVED to tell the story. I mean really, have you ever heard of someone who successfully went through cancer treatment being called a cancer victim? Nope. It's always survivor. Why is this any different?

If you experienced an awful and traumatizing situation, you're not a victim, you are a survivor.

I believe the smartest thing to do after a traumatic event is to embrace your survivor status as quickly as possible. You endured an immense physical and emotional challenge and came out the other side. Survivors inspire people and can teach from the wisdom gained in their experiences, just as the stories in this book do. Survivors are strong. Survivors

ROCK. If you are one out of five women and you are reading this, guess what? You are a survivor.

Victims receive sympathy.
Survivors inspire empathy.

BAD WORD: MONSTER

We like the word monster because it insinuates that the person is no longer human; they are nothing like us. We'd like to think that the rest of us human, non-monster types are all sunshine, rainbows and bunnies hopping through the meadow. A human would never do anything so dastardly. Well, we do. Constantly. Humans perpetrate deeply disturbing, shameful acts on each other all the time, every day around the globe. It's part of *being* human. As discussed in Section I, referring to a criminal as a monster elevates him into an inhuman category which we have no defenses for.

This is a very bad concept to try to work with when it's already hard enough to contain natural fear about fighting an opponent. News outlets would like nothing more than to scare the crap out of you with gruesome, sensational details to guarantee you'll sit through the commercials to catch the whole story. Resist the urge to let media rent space in your brain. When it comes to fear-based news, they're just high paid carnival barkers that read teleprompters.

BETTER WORD: CRIMINAL

The man who committed these acts broke the law and is therefore a criminal. This man is nothing more than a person who has demonstrated that he's not capable of living in society. Avoid him. And if he grabs you, you are strong enough to fight back. End of story.

WORDS IN PERSPECTIVE

Although I propose using alternative words to empower yourself and help make discussion more accessible for survivors, it's also important that we 'get over' these words. Like a school yard bully that thrives on intimidating you, the moment to stand up for yourself, their hold on you goes away. Replacing and/or 'getting over' these words will help eliminate unnecessary fear and hopefully allow you to also rethink the word so it never charges you with fear again.

Don't allow any word to send you into an emotional tail spin.

Some dubious people assume certain words will scare you. They're counting on it. They will use them as a manipulation tool to separate you from your power. Be aware if you are avoiding certain words because they are still pushing you against the lockers and stealing your lunch money.

If these or any other words bother you as they do some of the women in my seminars, write them and say them a thousand times or whatever you feel will help you desensitize yourself. Use them as armor to protect yourself. Replacing them is about changing your relationship with a concept so you can stay in your power, not avoiding them because they scare you.

Whenever you hear a news story about a monster, a predator rapist who is on the loose, decide to hear the story about yet another criminally disempowered man who you would consider an opponent if he decided to pick a fight with you. Instead of getting scared, get aware and walk down the street like you own the place.

SECTION III - Demystify The Criminal Mind

"If ignorant both of your enemy and yourself, you are certain to be in peril." - Sun Tzu

KNOW YOUR OPPONENT

☞ Who you think is a threat vs who actually is

☞ How boys become dangerous men

☞ Meet the personalities behind the crimes

This section is devoted to acquainting you with a very general psychological profile of the men perpetrating these crimes and help you see a small piece of their motivational puzzle. After each description of the criminals themselves, there is a breakdown of advantages, disadvantages and strategies to deal with each one.

Realize that it is virtually impossible to put a definitive label on any criminal thus impossible to create a strategy to deal with all of them. The only category that all criminals fit into is that they cannot be accurately contained in any single category. There are common behaviors, shared traits and similarities, but each individual has their own unique process and scenario which would require it's own unique safety solution.

It's important to understand who they are now and how they came to be. The idea is to make them more relatable so you can better cope with your concerns and fear about them.

A DIFFERENT ANIMAL

Realize who you're dealing with. The human brain is still quite un-evolved from our hunter-gatherer days, so the relationship between violence and sex in a man's brain is very close.

Not too long ago in evolutionary terms, men would fight each other for tribe domination and the right to mate with the alpha female. Immediately following their victory, they would copulate. In the animal kingdom, which we are a part of, this is still the tradition. Violence followed by sex is normal. As animals, men can be competitive, territorial and have violent tendencies that are behavioral echoes from our ancestral days. Women can be violent too, but violence is generally not our first instinct.

The important distinction from the perspective of self defense is violence against women is not about sex. It is about power. It is about taking power from someone so that the taker feels more powerful. Why sex? Because it is the sharpest most destructive weapon a coward has. In their eyes, it is the most complete violation. It forces the ultimate surrender. It is like crack to someone who feels powerless and out of control. And once they get a taste for it, it's a hard habit to break.

WHO ARE THESE GUYS?

This chapter focuses on a few general types of criminals who are out and about. You'll learn what motivates them and how they like to manipulate. You'll discover your advantages and disadvantages. Simply knowing this information can put you in a mental place of empowerment and increase the likelihood that you can successfully avoid trouble with these guys. Understanding the realities of who is potentially dangerous will keep your awareness where it needs to be instead of what slasher movies and the ten o'clock news are telling you.

Realize: 73% of survivors know their opponent. 93% of juvenile survivors know their opponents [7]. Stranger-danger crimes are more reported, more sensational, but statistically account for much less of the problem.

It's very important to be educated about the different varieties of criminally dysfunctional people walking around. This can help you recognize when bold action is needed to clearly demonstrate that you are going to be trouble and not worth the effort.

---

[7] Rape Abuse & Incest National Network: http://rainn.org/statistics

Understanding these types of criminals helps you see them when they're in front of you, even as they tell you that they are something else.

Although there are many different approaches to profiling, I'm a fan of the FBI rapist typology developed by their Behavioral Science Unit. The behavioral tendencies they list paint a vivid picture of the types of personalities behind violent crimes against women.

REMINDER: The advantages, disadvantages and strategy sections are to get you started with your mental training and beginning to think about a successful plan. It must be understood that there is no set solution; the only rule is that you can't make rules. The suggestions I make are but a few of the possible options. As you read, consider how you might handle an encounter with such a person.

THE LINE UP

You may have actually met one of these guys at some point in your life. This list is a fraction of some of the incarnations of power and control-hungry, angry criminal behavior you might encounter. Some of the following categories are based on the typology from the book Practical Aspects of Rape Investigation.[8]

---

[8] Practical Aspects of Rape Investigation: A Multidisciplinary Approach, Third Edition (Practical Aspects of Criminal & Forensic Investigations) edited by
Robert R. Hazelwood, Ann Wolbert Burgess

From now on, no person is beyond your scrutiny.

THE CONSIDERATE RAPIST

It sounds insane, but this criminal genuinely doesn't want to hurt the woman or himself while he is committing his crime. He's a watcher and a planner. He prefers to take advantage of a conveniently unlocked door or open window. This criminal will choose same age targets around his home. He's a shoe-in for the neighborhood peeping-Tom. He will study the habits and houses/apartments of his targets to ensure as little drama as possible in order to gain access to them. If the target typically locks their house up consistently, he will wait until they are out of the house and create an entry point that he will use later. He primarily sticks with strangers and fantasy rules his plan.

He is likely to threaten verbally and insinuate he has a weapon of some kind, but to brutally force or physically injure would ruin the mood.

He has fantasies about how much the target enjoys him and to satisfy himself he needs her to act like a willing participant. Unlike most other types of rapists, dehumanizing and demeaning his target is not the goal. The affirmation he seeks comes from getting his target to participate in the fantasy. He genuinely thinks of himself as her lover. He may share unsolicited personal details with his target and be full of compliments for her. It's not unusual for this guy to apologize and act like he cares. It's also not usual for this criminal to recontact the target via mail or phone after the incident, finding out how she is, asking for forgiveness or apologizing.

Your biggest advantage: He's counting on your fear and willingness to remain passive and compliant.

Disadvantage: Because he may only exert minimal force as needed to gain control of his target and acts somewhat reasonably the rest of time, it is confusing and can play to our instinct to cooperate.

A strategy for this opponent: His crime requires that you act your part in the fantasy. If you are non-compliant, provide plenty of verbal and possibly physical resistance, you may ruin his fantasy, his plan and facilitate his hasty exit.

DOMINANT CONTROL RAPIST:

This guy is out to prove his manhood by sexually abusing a woman and he doesn't care if he hurts her. He's a more of an impulsive opportunist and not a big planner so he strikes whenever it works for him. This is a wolf in sheep's clothing. He feels that forcing himself on a woman is his right. For this guy, rape is all about him flexing his manhood... which he feels he is entitled to do anytime he wants. It is likely you will meet this guy in a bar or at a party. Statistically, this type is of criminal contributes a significant number of the violent crimes against women. He might have had an ideal childhood but somehow managed to grow up with an arrogance and sense of entitlement that has made him dangerous.

He's the guy around your age who appears to be very nice at first. Buying you a drink at a bar, chatting you up at a cafe or offering to help put groceries in your trunk. He'll probably be polite, well groomed, educated, financially secure and social. As soon he senses that you have let your guard down, he pounces with both fists. He has no problem beating women into submission to accomplish his goal.

This guy typically doesn't use weapons since that would require a little more forethought than he is willing to give. If ever there was a date-rape poster child, it would be this guy. He's into degradation and dehumanization.

Your biggest advantage: You know he's out there. Even though he's trying to hide his agenda, he may be supremely confident, even a little arrogant, when he approaches. He will be seeking a target and may need to establish a connection to accomplish his goal. It can take a little time to gain your trust. You can see him coming.

Disadvantage: He may be very good at hiding his agenda. Especially if you are in a position that would make his approach logical (in a bar hoping to meet someone, needing a good samaritan, etc). He relies on his well groomed appearance, decent lifestyle and social graces to lull you into complacency.

A Strategy For This Opponent: If you are approached by a stranger for whatever reason, <u>keep your guard up</u> until you are in a safe place or surrounded by people you feel you can trust. Once secure, feel free to determine whether or not his demeanor is genuine. Consider not accepting help, rides, drinks or anything else a stranger offers. Remember, you don't owe strangers ANYTHING, including accepting their help. If they challenge your refusal, that's good evidence that they don't have your best interests in mind. Reminder: Just because someone is the same race and socio-economic class as you doesn't make them trustworthy or safe.

RETRIBUTION RAPIST:

This man has one mission: To make women pay. He is ANGRY. Whatever trauma has happened to him, he blames women. All women. He is a card carrying misogynist and yells it from the rooftops. He is not a planner, he is just working out blind rage on whatever unfortunate woman either reminds him of a female wrongdoer in his life or just has horrible timing. When this guy gets wound up, he immediately seeks a woman upon which to unleash his pent-up anger. His targets are usually around his age, maybe a few years his elder, and generally strangers. He is not a very common type to run into.

He lacks confidence so his favorite thing to do is sneak up and beat the hell out of a woman so she doesn't have a chance to defend herself. Because his anger makes him so eager to get relief, he will be bold, striking anytime of day or night and just about any location he can get away with. His intentions are purely punitive. To him, women are no more than an empty shell to receive the full extent of his brutal rage. He wants to degrade and dehumanize.

Your biggest advantage: Surprise is the lynch pin of his plan. You know he's out there and how he operates.

Disadvantage: He can come out of nowhere, on a mission, no hesitation, and assault his target when she least expects it. This is the "wrong place at the wrong time" type of scenario.

A Strategy For This Opponent: Awareness, awareness, awareness. This guy is a dangerous human animal. His kind is sure to set off all of your intuition alarms. If you are aware of your environment, willing to follow your gut and respond without hesitation, you will probably be able to avoid this guy.

RITUAL RAPIST:

The first thing to understand about this criminal is he is the least likely for you to encounter. Because his crimes will make the news and inspire books and movies, he is often the most feared. Good news: Despite his intelligence and cunning, he is still just a man with a plan. If you are practicing awareness, you drastically increase the likelihood that you can avoid or escape him.

Splashy headlines about these people leave us feeling terrified, but truth is, we're probably more likely to get hit by lightening than have to deal with this type of criminal because he is looking for something very specific. When he finds the woman who fits the bill (hair color, length, skin tone, build etc) then the ritualistic behavior is triggered.

He's a sadist so simply killing is not enough to satisfy his need. His satisfaction requires intense and prolonged fear from his chosen target. Often, he is raised by a single parent and has either been a direct recipient of horrendous abuse or witnessed it during his childhood. He is a little bit older, tending toward his early to late 30's. It's not unusual for him to be married with a family and to live in a good neighborhood. He is incredibly organized, college educated, and devotes a great deal of time to avoiding capture. Perhaps his greatest flaw is thinking he is much smarter than anyone who would try to catch him.

This is the kind of man who sweats the details and takes his time. Studying, tracking, planning. Clever, cruel and determined, something or someone stomped the humanity out of this person long ago. He will choose his targets outside of his area (house, work, etc.) and will have all the equipment needed in the trunk of his inconspicuous vehicle to execute his plan. This is the guy that all the neighbors describe as "nice" or "quiet". People don't think to look in plain sight for someone who is hiding.

He takes his targets to isolated areas. He will keep his targets detained for days or longer to maximize the dose of fear, control, power and superiority he needs to trip his trigger. He is a fear vampire, drinking in his targets terror like blood to nourish his twisted emptiness.

Ritual is extremely important to him and he will have planned the event in every detail, from the abduction to dumping the body.

He will be calm, like a surgeon, and once the ritualistic sequence begins, it ends the same way every time. The most important thing to realize about this type of opponent is, like a drunk or a person with a head injury, he cannot be reasoned with. Once the ritual has begun, there is no one behind the wheel.

This is the guy who could pass a polygraph after a brutal abduction and murder. Zero conscience. This man is beyond rehabilitation. Whatever trauma has robbed him of any shred of empathy or moral compass, his job is to be in jail where he can't hurt anyone.

He will use many different tactics to wear you down, get you to like, trust or feel sorry for him. These are manipulations; misdirections to keep you busy so you won't notice that he's finessing a proverbial noose around your neck.

The Ritual Rapist isn't the only offender who will try to convince you he's something he's not. Verbal manipulation is often part of their creepy plan. He may appear friendly, social, charming and intelligent, but he is *still a stranger who hasn't earned your trust.*

HI. I'M A RED FLAG

Here are some red flag behaviors designed to engage a target. Some of them are based on a behavior breakdown in Gavin De Becker's book <u>The Gift of Fear</u>:[9] A dangerous person may be hiding behind the following misdirection masks:

- He shares a lot of personal information in a short period of time without being asked
- Asks for your help or seems conspicuously helpless
- Showers you with compliments
- Invites himself to help you with something so you may feel obliged to return the favor
- Self-effaces by suggesting that he's probably not good enough for you to even talk to
- Insults you playfully to try to get you to refute his assertion and prove him wrong
- Ignores all of your refusals or your 'no's'
- Works the word 'we' into the conversation to imbue a sense of teamwork, association or being on your side
- Acknowledges your suspicions or unease with promises not to hurt you

---

[9] The Gift of Fear Survival Signals That Protect Us From Violence, Gavin De Becker, Little, Brown & Company, 1st edition

- Insists that he's harmless or that he's not dangerous
- Assures you that you can trust him
- Wants to get you alone (in a car, inside your apartment/house, isolated area)
- Takes social liberties (like teasing) that aren't appropriate for someone who doesn't know you
- Has a female companion and requests your assistance which requires getting close to a vehicle, isolated area or away from other people

Each tactic is a different route to the same result: To get you off your guard. To distract you.

To some extent, Ted Bundy falls into this category. His classic M.O. was needing help. He would don an arm cast or crutches or just ask for assistance. He was very attractive, confident, highly intelligent and one charming SOB.

These men are particularly dangerous because they are so amiable, we instinctively want to return the niceness. They are skilled at playing on our communal, cooperative instincts. The last thing on our minds will be that we need to treat him like the dangerous, wild human animal he is.

Your biggest advantage: His targets are selected by specific criteria which reduces the candidate pool to a very small number. If you are aware that you are in his process, you may be able stop it with powerful verbal resistance alone because it may ruin his game. Once he's been outed, it's much harder for him to convince you to let your guard down and it's much more difficult to abduct a suspecting, non-surprised target. Also, the longer you verbally and physically protest, the more you interfere with his ritual.

Disadvantage: Planning and surprise. He's smooth as silk and may not seem dangerous unless you know what you're looking for. He uses his charm and confidence like nerve gas. Generally these men are very smart and probably attractive. Single women looking to meet men are particularly vulnerable.

A strategy for this opponent: Accept that he exists. Realize that despite all of his scary plans, he is just a man. A man with multiple areas on his body that are vulnerable to simple strikes like every other man. This is an opponent who will most likely require no holds-barred physical and verbal resistance. Keep in mind, when Ted Bundy posed as a police officer and tried to abduct a woman at a Utah mall parking lot, she fought and got away. She had no special training and she escaped from TED BUNDY. You could escape this kind of criminal too if you keep your wits about you and you do not hesitate to defend yourself.

INTUITION NOTE: You will *not want to believe* and most likely deny the fact that this 'nice guy' has horrific plans that you need to ruin immediately and loudly. He can be intuition kryptonite because he'll give you every rationalization you need to talk yourself out of listening to your instincts.

Awareness is your most effective weapon. Be aware if you suddenly have a constant companion, whom you've never met, showing up at regular intervals or if someone unknown to you has taken an interest or trying to talk to your friends to get information about you. Open a space in your brain for the possibility that a seemingly harmless observer or sudden new charming acquaintance could pose a great threat. Consider involving the police as soon as possible and get their advice on the safest way to proceed.

Err on the side of *too much caution* if you suspect that a stranger has taken an unsolicited interest in you. If you're wrong, worst case scenario you may owe someone an apology or look a little foolish. If you're right, you may save your own life and those of countless other women. This is the time we live in. Accept it and move forward.

⚠ TRUE STORY

This happened to me when I was living in Westwood, home of UCLA, in a really cool mid-century modern apartment building. Only 12 units and a common entrance that was never locked. One afternoon, while my husband was out running errands, there was a knock on the door. I looked through the peep-hole and saw a 20ish, white, college-student-looking young man standing there. I asked him what he wanted and he said he had something for our upstairs neighbors that he wanted to give me, to give to them. Since our upstairs neighbors were good kids (scholarships, great parents, etc) who had a constant stream of relatively polite, respectful friends in and out, it tracked for me and I opened the door.

He apologized for the ruse, said he was actually selling magazines but that "my neighbors said that I was nice and wouldn't mind... isn't that right?" I really disliked being manipulated to gain access to me so I said, "No. I'm not nice." I watched the color drain from his face as I shut the door on him.

I don't know what he actually wanted and I didn't care. I noticed, however, that he didn't have any magazines, clip board or any other thing that would support his "real" reason for knocking on my door. Strangers may or may not get to talk with me, depending on the situation. Strangers who lie to me definitely do not get to talk to me.

GARDEN VARIETY OPPORTUNISTS:

These are the loiters, the 'last call' operators at bars, the trollers and the jogging trail lurkers. In terms of stranger danger, you are more likely to run into one of these guys. They are disgruntled, they feel disempowered and they want some of yours. They sometimes make the news because their intended target successfully fought them off.

Some are more dangerous than others, but they tend to strike in a few common scenarios: You are distracted, wearing headphones or have impaired judgement.

When you hear stories of joggers getting jumped, intoxicated girls being taken advantage of, these are the guys. They're looking for the easy mark.

These criminals know what they're doing is wrong, they just don't think they will get caught. When they do get caught, they can take responsibility and will feel remorse.

Your biggest advantage: They are looking for really easy targets or relying on surprise. No clever manipulations or too much planning. When you tell them to get the hell away from you or put up a good fight, they will generally go away.

Disadvantage: They lurk in places where women are comfortable, complacent and tend to be more likely to be good targets.

The strategy for this opponent: Awareness and assertiveness. By letting them know that you see them, you know what they're up to and you are ready to make a scene if need be, that alone may provide enough evidence that you are not a good target and they'll look elsewhere.

⚠ TRUE STORY

This happened to me when I was living in Denver, CO. I was out jogging one afternoon with my headphones on. As cars passed, I noticed that one car slowed down as it went by. It made me uncomfortable. It was moving so slow I was able to note the make, model, color, partial license plate and that there was only one person in the car. A man with a full head of dark brown straight hair. I watched him take the first right turn he could and I just <u>knew</u> that I would see that car again on the next block. Sure enough, as I jogged past the next intersection, there he was, waiting for me.

Without thinking, I slowed down to a walk, made eye contact and pointed at him as I went by. Although I hadn't planned it, the message was 'I see you'. His tires squealed as he sped off.

Afterwards, I remember thinking, what the hell? Why did I point at that man like I was his first grade teacher? Then I realized I didn't have to understand. Instead of feeling silly for essentially shaking my finger at a random male driver, I felt lucky to have been given such strong, clear direction from my intuition and for listening to it.

CRIMINAL MUSTER

Whenever you are approached by a stranger or even an acquaintance wanting your time, attention, help or offering to help, determine if they pass a litmus test. Ask yourself:

1. What does my gut say about this person right now? Am I uncomfortable?
2. Are they respecting my polite refusal? (a decent person with honorable intentions will listen to you; respect your boundaries and acknowledge your right to say no)
3. Have I lost track of the fact that this stranger/someone I barely know is trying to convince me to do something? Or allow him to do something?
4. Do I have any idea what this person is capable of?

Remember that the most psychopathic criminals are least likely to cross our paths. The majority of men creating the problem are acquaintances. The bad news is we tend to be emotionally tied to them or trust them and more likely to *let* them mistreat us. The good news is the moment we realize it's not right and give them resolute verbal resistance, they tend to move on.

ACQUAINTANCE ADVANTAGE

73% of *all assaults* come from non-strangers.[10]

Behold the heart of the problem. These are generally the boys and men we date, our boyfriends, male friends etc. This section deals with men who are trusted and familiar to us, who suddenly reveal themselves as dangerous during a date or other interaction.

The good news about this staggering statistic is that it is so utterly preventable. It can be prevented through clear communication and by being prepared to take action. Then, we must educate our daughters, sisters, cousins and friends how to do the same.

Your biggest advantage: They assume you want them to like you and that's their big leverage. When you verbally resist, showing them that you are more concerned about you than being liked by them, they lose their leverage and their power to manipulate you.

---

[10] Rape Abuse & Incest National Network: http://rainn.org/statistics

Disadvantage: When a woman's self-esteem is low, fear of loneliness and lack of self-worth can open the door for opportunistic people. At the point when the situation turns dangerous, women tend to deny it and remain compliant because they don't want to drive the man away with rejection. The compulsion to care about the needs of someone who doesn't treat them well may already be firmly in place when these situations arise. A significant change in perspective and a solid support system is needed to emotionally re-prioritize and advocate for oneself.

The toughest obstacle to overcome is recognizing and accepting the fact that your boyfriend or male acquaintance has just become your opponent. Going there mentally can help prevent having to go there physically. The sooner you can prepare yourself for this possibility, the better you will be at ending a bad relationship before it goes that far or protecting yourself if necessary.

The strategy for this opponent: The second you get uncomfortable, you must stop the momentum and be clear that you are uncomfortable. Offer a firm 'NO'. Once this break in the mood has occurred, do not let yourself be convinced to give in.

A WORD ABOUT INCEST

According to current statistics, [11] 93% of juvenile survivors knew their abusers, 34% were family, 58% were acquaintances.

Incest is a much more complicated topic. Although the legal lines are clearer, it's so taboo that no one wants to talk about it. Incest is much less common in adults and the topic of child molestation already has many excellent books with which to educate yourself.

Since abuse in the home can result in criminal activity as adults, this is a topic everyone should learn more about. Even if you don't have children, if you become aware of an abusive situation you have the power to stop it. This is an opportunity for everyone to help stop the cycle of violence.

There are lots of resources, like Stop It Now (www.stopitnow.org), that detail warning signs and behaviors in children and adults. Someone else's abused child may not be your problem now, but they could be when they grow up damaged, angry and looking for relief.

Being aware of the child abuse process may allow you see something that no one else is able to see and if appropriate, start the wheels of intervention turning.

---

[11] Rape Abuse & Incest National Network: http://www.rainn.org/statistics

THE STRAW THAT BROKE THE CAMEL'S BRAIN

This chapter is devoted to examining the factors that can contribute to innocent boys growing up to become dangerous men.

Here is the problem:
There are mentally unstable, emasculated, broken boys and men everywhere. The Hurt often go on to hurt others.

They hang out in bars, work in offices, run companies, loiter on street corners, go to school and lead normal lives. At some point, usually when they were young boys, someone traumatized them deeply. Someone may have humiliated, neglected and/or physically abused them. Most people develop coping mechanisms and persevere despite deep emotional wounds. Other people are irreparably broken by their childhood traumas.

Without a proper strategy, intervention nor psychological ability to cope with their emotional distress, they are on the hunt for something to make themselves feel better. A salve that will bring them comfort, that will fill the void, albeit temporary. Reliving their own trauma through the eyes of the person dishing, rather than taking. They are physically strong but emotionally weak. They will continue to act out this sociopathic loop their mind has created in lieu of valid coping mechanisms until they are caught, killed or seek help.

WHAT THE HECK IS GOING ON??

Here's a very meaningful glimpse into the psyche of men. Once again, from Gavin DeBecker[12]:

The deepest fear of men is to be laughed at by a woman. The deepest fear of women is to be killed by a man.

That comparison indicates, among other things, that men equate humiliation with death. Worse than death. This incredible insight explains a lot about what men value. In a very general sense, women can get validation internally whereas men tend to rely on the external.

A common theme among sexual criminals is that most of them come from disturbed childhoods and one of the most destructive forces is maternal neglect. Additionally, they learned about violence by either being physically/emotionally abused themselves and/or witnessing abuse in their household. The common denominator is feeling tremendous fear and powerlessness as a child. Reminder: rape is a crime of power and control, not sex.

Depending on what age they were abused, the type of abuse, gender of and relationship with of the abuser, a different type of violent adaptation can result.

---

[12] The Gift of Fear Survival Signals That Protect Us From Violence, Gavin De Becker, Little, Brown & Company, 1st edition

Does that give them the right to abuse others? Definitely NOT.

Knowing that fact sheds some light on the cycle of violence. Our plight is not the result of random acts of the amoral or disgruntled. These men were born innocent children. They were regular kids until they were literally ruined by traumatic events that were continually heaped upon them until their young spirits were crushed and their humanity along with it.

A consistent source of violence against women is neglect and violence toward impressionable boys.

One solution for the problem begins by interfering with the genesis of the problem.

THE CYCLE OF VIOLENCE BEGINS

The process of boys developing into dangerous men is very simplified here and only accounts for a few of the contributing factors. There are many variations and this information is not complete by any means. The following information is meant to show the connection between parent's issues and how they can impact boys in destructive and sometimes permanent ways.

There are many common factors among dangerous, broken men. One is that the abuse occurred before the age of seven, which is considered by many the age of reason. Knowing right from wrong. When children are abused before age seven, while the brain is still making crucial connections, it can lead to changes in brain chemistry that result in actual brain damage. Sometimes this permanent damage cannot be treated with pharmaceuticals or behavioral rehabilitation.

Childhood abuse can create emotional injuries so severe they suppress normal brain development, resulting in damage that can be seen on MRI.

I can't emphasize enough that this section may be hard for some people to read. It's not meant to cast blame or point fingers, just inform. If you don't know what you don't know, you cannot be blamed for unintentional mistakes. Also, there many, many factors that can contribute to a boy growing into an abusive man. It's rarely just one isolated event that that ruins someone. Repetitive abuse results in a poor self image that creates fertile ground for becoming a threat to others.

This is a look through the keyhole, at a particular stage of development, as an example of where mothers and other care takers can potentially deeply impact the young psyche of a boy.

Take a moment to remember the deepest fear of a man. To be laughed at. To be humiliated. When a man is at his most vulnerable, the power to shape his opinion of himself is in someone else's hands. Especially when he is in love.

**A boys first love and his deepest bond tends
to be with his mother.**

Boys want their mother to love them no matter what. She
has super-hero powers in his eyes. She is his world. Same for
girls and fathers. In fact, the kind of abuse that creates brain
damage in a girl is paternal physical or sexual abuse.
Psychologically speaking, the most destructive element in a
young boy's emotional development is maternal neglect.

In many ways, boys can be much more sensitive than girls.
They may prefer trucks to dolls and wrestling to tea parties,
but they can be emotionally tender. I've witnessed this with
my friends' children.

All kids go through many phases as they mature. For very
young children, the anal stage, which is defined by toilet
training (2-3 years old), and the phallic stage (3-5 years old)
which is defined by boys figuring out that their penis is the
greatest thing on earth, are potentially delicate times.

On the surface, it's pretty basic stuff. The trouble starts when
these vulnerable phases are met with anger, violence, shame
or humiliation.

THREATS + HUMILIATION + SHAME = VIOLENCE

When a boy discovers how wonderful it is to have a penis, if
his behavior is met with violence and threats, it can create an
unhealthy connection between violence and natural sexual

arousal. This sets the stage for big, bad problems. Some men report that their mothers or grandmothers threatened them when they would touch themselves.

"If I catch you touching that, I will cut it off!" is a common threat.

The boys completely believe these threats to be real. They are terrified.

By creating an environment of shame, humiliation, fear and violence around their son's natural sexual urges, those feelings can become linked with one another.

This scenario can result in arrested emotional development, particularly with regard to a boy's sexual maturation.

Have you ever wondered what could possibly motivate a man to sexually assault a senior citizen? If Grandma regularly used threats of violence to control a boy's behavior, it makes complete sense that he might grow up with a vendetta against elderly women.

THE DAMAGE UNFOLDS

When a boy is nine or ten years old, he may begin to act out by abusing animals, as Jeffery Dahmer did. During adolescence, these boys have an overactive sense of entitlement and invulnerability. More so than typical teens.

They won't be told 'no' and become fearless. They are already potentially dangerous to girls their age or younger. When the urge to explore sex increases with puberty, their brain can't reconcile their feelings.

A scared, humiliated boy is trapped in a growing man's body filled with frustration, anger and increasing levels testosterone.

In an abusive environment, low self opinion can lead to habitual need to prove oneself, which can include forcing sex. Damaged boys act out the pain they feel about their sexuality.

Their normal urges have been twisted into something shameful and forbidden and they have no healthy way to deal with their burgeoning manhood. The likelihood of rehabilitation depends on the individual's ability to recover, the severity and duration of abuse and the age at which intervention begins.

THE CYCLE OF VIOLENCE IN MOTION

A boy is grows up in an abusive household, he is wounded, fearful and angry. As a man, he doesn't have the capacity to relate to women in a healthy way. He acts out his aggression by forcing himself on women. The wounded woman develops deep self-worth problems and issues around sex. She goes onto to marry an abuser and has a son, who naturally discovers his penis at some point, which triggers her issues about sex and she acts out by punishing him for touching himself. He grows up damaged and punishes women by forcing sex, who go on to act out their issues on their sons and so on, and so on, and so on...

Granted, it's far more complicated than that and there are innumerable variables that can take that cycle in different directions, but you get the idea. This is one thread out of thousands in a complex behavior fabric, but it is one thread we can impact directly.

HERO WORSHIP

Another area where mothers may be inadvertently dropping the ball is with highly talented athletic sons. There is a very strong relationship between successful athletes and violence against women. Often these young men may have had wonderful childhoods. Their mothers tirelessly support them as they blossom into collegiate or even professional caliber players. As they become more valuable to their high school teams, the spotlight gets bigger and brighter.

They are courted by impressive, winning college programs and they become elevated pack leaders in their social groups. Every boy wants to be their friend and every girl wants them to pick her. It grooms our youth to feel entitled to get whatever they want, *whenever* they want it and for their sycophantic followers to enable them, lest they loose their precious affiliation. They can do no wrong and those that profit from them (coaches, schools, communities and even parents) protect them at all costs.

When these kids are faced with pressures and opportunities that even adults would struggle with, having only their tenuous adolescent morality to guide their choices and a deep sense of infallibility, bad things can happen. Their sense of entitlement or sense of responsibility can come from their mother's insistence. Think of all the good that could come from teaching them to be a star *and* a role model. Even boys "raised right" by aware, empowered women will make stupid, dangerous or even deadly choices as they careen through their burgeoning pubescence into manhood. That said, the amount of sway that mothers hold over their sons can't be underestimated.

Men learn what they know as boys. Mother's have an opportunity to teach boys many things, good and bad.

ONE SOLUTION STARTS WITH WOMEN TAKING ACTION

I could go on all day long about the responsibility of men and fathers, but as far as Unbreakable Woman is concerned, its irrelevant because we can only control what WE contribute to the equation. We must stay focused on what women have the power to change.

As mothers, we help shape kid's opinions about themselves. As girlfriends and wives, we give men feedback as to how we expect to be treated.

We must look beyond any past guilt or resist the temptation to blame others for what's happened in our lives. If we have been traumatized by sexual violence, we have a choice in how we respond. We choose how we want to live the rest of our lives. It's important to own those choices and stay empowered.

It's time that we put the focus firmly on what we can control: How we behave, who we choose to share our lives with, how we treat others and how we *let* ourselves be treated. This teaches our children what they need to know.

It's very important that we treat our young boys with the same respect we expect them to give to women in the future. If we intimidate them to control behavior, guess what we're teaching them? The bigger, stronger person gets what they want through intimidation.

Recognize that boys can be very emotionally sensitive so being neutral and supportive during their more vulnerable developmental stages can contribute to a healthy self image.

We need to be the protectors of these boys so they can feel that their most vulnerable, sacred areas are safe. The male psyche is just as open to trashing as the female. When they're young, maybe even more so. Boys with special abilities need to understand that with great power, comes great responsibility. Walk the walk. Insist on being treated with respect and consideration by your boyfriend or spouse. This teaches your son how to treat women. How will he learn to respect women if you don't *show him how* you respect yourself?

⚠ TRUE STORY

Toilet training and "genital discovery management" are part of how we train young, undomesticated human animals to live in civilized society. Some of the best parenting I have ever witnessed was when the 4 year-old daughter of a dear friend of mine was going through her discovery phase and humping everything she was tall enough to straddle.

One morning, my friend found her young daughter gleefully humping the living room couch and she matter-of-factly said, "Honey, what you're doing is natural, but that's something you need to do in your room, not the living room. So you have a choice, you can go upstairs or sit properly on the couch." To which her daughter replied, "B" and proceeded to sit 'like a lady.'

Brilliant. My friend was so careful not to introduce shame or drama into the conversation nor did she try to stop a normal, healthy process that would eventually end just as naturally as it began.

It's easy for these natural phases to stir up the mud in the waters of our past issues. It's tricky but completely possible to educate children about social propriety without engendering shame and humiliation for a behavior driven by a natural, human urge. Same goes for hitting. It's natural for kids who lack verbal skills to lash out with their fists to communicate. Like all other childhood phases, if handled with calm, firm assertion, it's less likely to create a problem down the road.

I believe that parenting is the single, biggest challenge in life, and the most important. Having to maintain patience when you're ready to go medieval can push anyone to the brink. But healthy societies rely on parents raising decent humans beings who respect themselves and the rights of others.

Be aware if you're child's behavior during toilet training or genital discovery phase is emotionally triggering you. Take whatever steps you need to ensure that your children, both sons and daughters, grow up feeling like their sexuality is normal, healthy and special.

THE DATE TALK

Communicating clearly with your date is essential in preserving your emotional and physical well being as you are getting to know someone. Although this subject is worthy of a book of its own, sufficed to say that simple communication changes can make a quick course correction when you feel a date veering into uncomfortable territory.

START A DATE WITH YOU IN MIND

Here are two simple guidelines to keep in mind before going on dates.

1. You get to say 'no', anytime, anywhere to anyone. NO MATTER WHAT.

The only tricky thing about this guideline is you have to mean it. Be willing to back it up with physical resistance. If you're not ready to make your point physically, then perhaps 'no' is not what you mean to say. If you're not sure about how far you're interested in going, don't leave it up to a to a man to decide for you. Unless you're in a healthy, equitable relationship built on mutual trust and respect, guess what he'll choose?

If you mean to slow things down, say exactly that. Reserve 'no' for when you really mean 'stop' and consider saying 'stop' instead.

Saying 'no' repeatedly when you don't mean it dilutes the power of your words and reduces your credibility. People will stop believing that you mean what you say and won't take your requests seriously.

2. Communicate CLEARLY to prevent confusion on his part. Confusion is a bigger problem than you might think.

Say what you want and what you don't want. The more clear you are, the clearer his intentions will be if he decides he's going to try something you have said you aren't interested in. How can you or he know if he's crossing the line if you haven't clearly drawn it?

RAPE V NON-CONSENSUAL SEX

According to the judicial system, there is a difference between rape and non-consensual sex. If someone you know forces themselves upon you (with the exception of a family member), it falls into the non-consensual sex category versus a stranger which is considered rape or criminal sexual assault. If you know the man and there is any consensual contact prior to the rape, that makes it a lesser crime. They're prosecuted differently. Tell that to a survivor. The betrayal of a trusted person is many ways much worse than that of a stranger, but that's not how the justice system sees it. Sometimes it's hard to be clear when we ourselves are confused about what we want and what is good for us.

When it comes to sex, when in doubt, stop. If you regret not doing something, you can always do it the next time, but you can't undo something once it's done.

Because our culture showers us in an oil slick of guilt and shame about our sexuality, many women feel ashamed of their healthy sexual desires. We say 'no' so we don't feel like a slut even though we don't want to stop. It's yet another rotten gift from our pseudo-puritanical, hyper-sexualized culture that keeps on giving. This confusion and ambiguity is natural given all the mixed messages we get. Unfortunately, all this confusion can be dangerous.

One of the most common defenses of the boys or men who've been accused of non-consensual sex is that they were "confused." Given the unlikelihood of hormone saturated young males stopping themselves once they think sex is imminent, I imagine it would require specific and focused verbal resistance to clear up any "confusion" they were having.

Although I get that confusion may be an element in non-consensual sex...please people. With rare exception, "confusion" is a very convenient excuse for lack of respect for another person, laser-like focus on *their* needs and inability or unwillingness to control themselves.

<u>A smart policy to live by:</u>

Make up your mind what you're comfortable with BEFORE you even step out of the door. Tell your date about it. Stick to it. Respect your plan.

Tell your date/boyfriend/acquaintance etc. about your boundaries before you start making out. If you are willing to defend your plan verbally, chances are he will also respect it. Yes, it bursts the romance bubble a little, but doesn't ruin an evening like having to face doing something you really don't want to because you're afraid you can't stop the train.

Also, being clear from the beginning can help your date be more responsible with himself. For example, if he knows that there will be no sex of any kind, he can gauge how much physical contact he can handle before things start to get, shall we say, physically uncomfortable for him. Remember that intense sexual arousal without release can be intensely painful for men.

Having a plan decreases risk, however I understand that some women live for the rush of spur of the moment spontaneity. Naturally, the riskier scenarios seem like the most fun. I would never judge another woman's choice to do something dangerous since I've taken some pretty big, ridiculous risks in my life. Somehow, I was conscious that it could have all gone horribly wrong and was prepared to act. You must understand that spontaneity comes with a price and you need to keep you wits about you.

If you decide to introduce alcohol or drugs into the equation, be prepared to lose touch with crucial skills like intuition, good judgement and the ability to control your situation. If that is what you want, then go for it. But enter into that scenario with your eyes wide open.

<u>SECTION IV - Hone Your Skills</u>

"The only real valuable thing is intuition." - Albert Einstein

SIX CRITICAL SKILLS

☞ Understand The Skills You Already Have

☞ Learn How To Maximize Their Effectiveness

☞ Practice Them Regularly

In this chapter you'll explore how you've already got what it takes to defend yourself. Below are some life-preserving skills you probably didn't even know you had.

Unlike physical techniques that are easily lost if not practiced regularly in a specialized environment, the following native skills can be practiced every day, anytime, everywhere.

The only thing you need to do is be prepared to use these everyday skills and commit 100% in the event that you do.

Here's what you've got in your weapons cache:

1. *Awareness*

2. *Intuition*

3. *Boundaries*

4. *Assertiveness*

5. *Powerful Speech*

6. *Intentional Crazy*

These skills are available to you right now. When utilized, they greatly reduce the probability of needing to defend yourself physically.

Let's start from the beginning and detail each skill one by one.

AWARENESS

This is your first line of defense.

Intuition is always looking out for you, but will you be distracted and miss the signal?

What's going on around you and more importantly *who* is going on around you?

Cell phones, deadlines, commuting in bad weather, family drama. It's all part of our modern life and makes it hard to get out our heads. Being aware means being present. It's not about being paranoid and hyper vigilant, walking around in a fighting stance, eyes darting back and forth faster than watching a Williams sisters tennis match.

Awareness is about keeping a small portion of your attention reserved for observation of what and who is around you *at all times.* Casual surveillance is crucial.

Even if you're out to dinner with friends, as you enjoy yourself, you can glance at who's coming and going, the people at the tables around you, emergency exits, etc. This simple act can instantly connect you with your intuition. In a way, you are connecting with your environment, putting yourself in it, being present.

Awareness opens the door to your intuition and will provide feedback that you can use immediately, rather than having it jolt you out of a distracted state.

By glancing around, no matter where you are or what you're doing, you're actively and consciously seeking feedback. If there's something or someone around who your pings your intuition, you'll know about it with enough time to decide if any action is necessary.

Simply being aware that a situation has unknown elements that you may have to deal with will help you stay present and able minded. Whether on a date, on your cell while walking down the street, waiting at a stop light or putting groceries in your car, you'll know what is going on around you.

Always practice casual observation of your surroundings. Get a read on those around you and be prepared to act on any intuitive response you may get from your surveillance.

Remember: all it takes is conscious breathing to drop into the present.

INTUITION

This is your animal instinct. There are ancient structures in our brains that haven't changed in thousands of years which make up our Limbic System. The Limbic System is responsible for your survival and evaluates incoming messages (visual, physical, emotional) to assess danger. When your intuitive center senses danger in your vicinity, it responds by sending you an instant message. It pings you.

When a person has gone morally and psychologically off grid and is working on animal instincts, your intuition (survival instincts) will get triggered.

The great news about these intuitive signals is three fold:

1 - They are designed specifically to give you time to remove yourself from danger. In other words, they are your cavalry arriving in time for you to save yourself. When you realize you're in danger, you still have time. You still have choices.

2 - Your intuition is responding to something. There's always a reason you get a ping. If you haven't already, look around

you and see who or what has thrown the alarm or just get moving and figure it out later.

3 - Your survival instincts are your bodyguard. They are there for you, always ready to help keep you safe.

The tricky thing about intuition is that our reasoning minds like to chime in, trying to figure out the what, why and who.

It may feel strange, but you must accept that sometimes you won't know exactly what or why you've been triggered.

You don't need to. The trigger comes from your non-thinking survival nature. Our easily distracted thinking minds are way behind the ball. Be willing to follow your intuitive guidance even if it seems illogical.

Intuition can be incredibly subtle, for example you notice someone or turn to look over your shoulder, which is why the first pings are often overlooked. These small moments can be your indication to pay extra close attention. It's the "noticing" or "sudden urge" to turn your head that could be coming straight from your survival center. Understand that your intuition may begin with a whisper, but that doesn't make the information any less critical than a loud, flashing warning light.

WARNING: ALCOHOL AND DRUGS ARE INTUITION NAPALM

The more you ingest, the less you'll care. If you want to go there and do that, feel free. Enjoy. So long as you choose it consciously while understanding and accepting the risks.

BOUNDARIES

This is a very important part of your successful self defense. It's where you put your trip wires so you know if someone is trespassing.

If you go out into the world without a clear idea of where your physical, verbal and emotional boundaries are, how will you know if someone is venturing into your personal space?

Like the bumper sticker says, "If you can read this, you're too close!" Spend some quality time thinking about or discussing with trusted allies what kind of physical contact is okay with you and under what circumstances. It's something you can always reevaluate and change so I suggest erring on the side of conservative.

Once in place, be as clear and direct as possible with your comfort level and own it. You get to define your comfort zones any way you want.

Realize that sometimes harmless people, with different boundaries than you, may accidentally hit a trip wire with no ill intent.

And when it comes to being steadfast about where you draw your lines, the people who would tell you that you're too uptight probably don't have your best interest in mind. If they did, they would have more respect for your boundaries.

⚠ TRUE STORY

My husband and I are very physically expressive people. We tend to express our appreciation for friends new and old with warm hugs. We recently became friends with a wonderful couple. After meeting a few times for drinks, they invited us over for dinner and cooked a fabulous meal. We enjoyed talking about tons of topics and had a lot of fun. To express our appreciation, we hugged them on our way out. As we continued to spend time together, we always greeted them with enthusiastic hugs. We came to find out, through friends of the couple, that this couple never hugged ANYONE and were particularly non-touchy-feely people.

We were mortified to discover that we had crossed their personal physical boundaries, however unintentional. They were such nice people, they didn't want to make us feel bad so they didn't say anything. Needless to say, we stopped all attempts to hug them after that discovery. Although it is a little hard for me not to express my sincere adoration for them with an embrace, respecting their boundaries is more important. It never occurred to me to question why or judge them for our differences. My main concern was to nurture the friendship and respect their choices.

Healthy people will understand and respect your right to whatever boundaries you have chosen.

If someone is trespassing and you've been been crystal clear that they are making you uncomfortable, ask them to retreat. And if they don't, take it up a notch.

ASSERTIVENESS

Hi! Are you looking for something? Can I help you?

This is my FAVORITE tactic to handle a stranger lurking in my neighborhood. I live in a very community oriented part of the Northwest and it's quite obvious when someone who doesn't live in our 'hood is walking around looking for who knows what. Usually, it's an unarmed, bored, at-risk youth wandering around looking sheepish. I choose to engage them with the offer to help. It sounds like I'm being a helpful neighbor but the underlying message is clear: I don't recognize you and unless you are visiting one of my neighbors, there's no reason for you to be loitering in our alley. Once they realize they're not invisible, they usually make a hasty exit.

The intention behind your words is your power tool. Even the offer of help can be used to redirect a person with a dubious agenda.

This can be particularly useful when an unfamiliar person is about to cross your path. Sometimes brief eye contact, a nod or a casual "Hello" can let them know "I see you and I'm not afraid of you." It acknowledges without engaging and smells like confidence.

Assertiveness and confidence go hand in hand. One can help inspire the other. Walk with the confidence of someone who is ready and willing to stand up for themselves.

Make a pact with yourself that no matter what happens, the instant you feel something isn't right you will address it immediately. Either by avoiding the person if they're a distance away or verbally if you're face to face with whomever is making you uncomfortable.

Being assertive means you are present and willing to address what's in front of you. You are an active participant in what is going on around you all the time.

When something doesn't look, feel or sound right -- take action! It might be as simple as telling a waiter they brought the wrong entree. It might be as daunting as telling a suspiciously overly helpful stranger that you do not want their help putting your groceries in your trunk and they need to go away or you'll call the police.

Many women have a hard time making the transition from feeling a survival impulse to taking action because they don't want to seem like a bitch or it feels like an incredibly awkward and uncomfortable.

Our culture trains us to avoid the following at all costs: Causing a scene, making someone feel bad, experiencing the awkwardness of calling someone out on their dubious plan, being rude, being a bitch.

Someone who intends to harm you is <u>banking</u> on the fact that you won't say anything. They have already determined that you are the person who will just stand idly by and let them continue to walk deeper into unwelcome territory. Did they assess you correctly?

It takes some courage to overcome the adrenalin inducing moments before you take that first step into saying something you know will be unpopular or cause friction. Reminder: courage is not the absence of fear. Courage is taking action despite the fear.

It's not easy, but if you believe your personal safety is on the line, it will be much easier to make the other person aware that you have a problem with how they're treating you.

CHANGING THE WEATHER

This wonderful skill allows you to take advantage of cultural expectations. Changing the weather refers to every woman's ability to change her environment with a look, her energy and intention. For example, when you're around your friends and feeling safe, you're sunny and shining your light on everyone.

The moment someone traipses into your space in an unwelcome way, the sun goes away as the clouds start to form. Distant thunder can be heard and the unwelcome person will feel that lightening is about to strike. Even though your words are social or "nice", your energy is clear: back off.

We can tow the line of cultural expectation by being pleasant, even as we drop the temperature in a room to freezing.

POWERFUL SPEECH

Your voice is a powerful tool and an incredible ally. Once you learn how to harness it, you can put commanding power behind your words. Your words can provide warmth and support or penetrate the skin with icy daggers. Powerful speech is not just about what you say but how you say it.

To better understand the depth and breadth of this tool that you have at your disposal, I recommend taking a voice class.

A bellowing 'NO!' from the depths of your diaphragm can stop someone in their tracks. Learn how to bark so you won't have to bite.

Unlike physical skills, you can practice using your voice all the time so your self defense voice can be there when you need it.

SCRIPT BREAKING WITH YOUR VOICE

Sometimes, a criminal expects to hear certain things. They are waiting to hear the usual protest, like a dog with a squeaky toy. Part of their game is to dehumanize you, making it easier to carry out their plan.

For certain situations, verbalizing exactly what the criminal is doing and that there will be consequences may help break the script. Sometimes intuition gives you the words.

I heard a true story in one of my self defense classes about a wife and mother in her mid-50's who was walking home with groceries one day when a man came from out of nowhere and pounced. He tried to drag her into an alley. During the struggle, she noticed he had a hole in his jacket. She said, "Wait, you have a hole in your coat. You should give it to me so I can mend it for you." He let her go and ran off. When interviewed after the fact, she had no idea why she even noticed the hole or said what she said. Her intuition guided her in that moment.

This is a brilliant example of script breaking. As he dragged her into the alley, she yelled and protested. These were the sounds of his plan that he expected to hear, until she offered to mend his coat. Instantly, she went from a grey blob of nondescript meat to a vivid, living, breathing being. She had no special training and still managed to escape. This is exactly how women are powerful when they use their intuition. Her inner guidance told her the one thing that would neutralize her opponent without ever making a fist. No thinking, just pure instincts.

OVERCOMING CULTURAL OBSTACLES

In the seconds that you realize you need to say something because your safety depends on it, it's very tempting to back away from your verbal resistance. Apologizing for being assertive, in a way. It's how we're trained in this society. Our cultural conditioning to be liked is so deeply hard wired, we don't want to be rude, even when our life is in danger. It's preposterous. We may recognize and acknowledge that a situation has become uncomfortable, or even dangerous, then back down with statements like, "It's not your fault, it's me. I'm sorry, I'm just being paranoid." or "Please don't be offended" etc.

Your heart is in the right place, but you're caring about the wrong person.

Women are uncomfortable in this area so we try to soften our rejection. This may be appropriate when dealing with a well meaning, decent person, but not with a criminal who has already established themselves as not worthy of this nicety.

Being nice is a social convention and a choice. Get comfortable with the idea that that there are people who have not earned your kindness.

Just like a dog protesting when another tries to dominate it. You're *supposed* to provide negative feedback in some situations.

If someone has busted through your boundary trip wire, all bets are off. Use powerful language and don't back away from it. Commit.

Your opponent will try to convince you that you're wrong and may mistake nice for weak.

After telling someone 'No thank you' in so many ways and they are repeatedly ignoring your 'no', it may be time to make really clear, definitive statements that leave no room for misinterpretation. These examples are the equivalent of bearing your teeth, ears pinned back and growling.

"I didn't ask for your help. I DON'T WANT YOUR HELP!"
"I said I'm not interested. LEAVE ME ALONE!"
"I said NO! I will call the police if you don't go away!"

Here's a list of some phrases that escalate the ones above and clearly indicate you have drawn the line. The first word is to be exploded from your belly like a cannon to snap your opponent out of his script and give the words that follow some gravitas so there is no doubt you are capable and willing to bite if necessary:

1. **HEY!** Back off.

2. **STOP**! I'm calling the cops!
3. **NO**! Leave now.

YELLING FOR HELP

The best word to yell is FIRE!

- FIRE: With a good set of lungs and a properly supported yell, it can be recognizably heard up to about 1/4 mile. This word can be very effective if you are in a physical confrontation. Fire effects everyone and people will come out to see where the fire is. No kidding. Yell fire.

- NO: Always a good choice because it's so empowering, the same in many languages and clearly delivers your unwillingness to participate. That's a great word especially if the confrontation hasn't gotten physical. Will it get people to come help? Possibly.

- RAPE and HELP: Poor choices for a couple of reasons. One, because they cannot be yelled effectively. The 'P' sound is a plosive or stop consonant and requires you to stop the flow of air by putting your lips together then suddenly releasing it. Those sounds can't be verbally elongated or shouted, only the sounds before and after the letter can. When yelled, these two words don't travel very far and translate as 'ray' and 'el' from a distance. The second reason is that in our sadly, cynical culture people will close the curtains and turn up the TV if they hear a woman yelling either one of those words.

⚠ TRUE STORY

When I lived in a dicey East Hollywood neighborhood, one afternoon a man wandered into my bungalow complex. First he harassed one of the Armenian residents who didn't speak English before finding his way to my doorstep. I only had the screen door between him and me. He was about 6'2", 200 lbs, 30 something. It wasn't even 10:00 am and he reeked of alcohol. Drunk people do stupid things. My alarm bells went off. He was polite and asked me to read his screenplay. Only in LA... I returned his politeness and told him I didn't have time. He asked again, pleading with me to get my opinion, insisting another set of eyes would really help him out. A ridiculous request given that he did not know anything about me or my eyes. I declined again, more insistently. After his third attempt to enter my apartment with this cockamamy story, I squared my body to him and told him calmly, "I feel like you are not hearing my 'no'. When you ignore my 'no' it makes me feel like you are a danger to me and I need to call the police. Do I need to call the police?" He left.

Tools used:

-   Awareness: Being aware of what was happening outside my apartment allowed me to observe his behavior before he got to my door and alerted me to the fact that he was trouble.

-   Intuition: My survival instinct "morning drunk guy is dangerous," made it easier to transition to verbal resistance.

- Assertiveness: My willingness to talk about exactly what was happening in the moment.

- Powerful Speech: Clearly letting him know that I was not going to be a participant in whatever fantasy he he had concocted and thankfully it broke the script that was running in his head.

And one of my sassy female neighbors eventually yelled, "Get out of here! I'm calling the cops." Same idea, same result, different delivery.

That's what basic assertiveness is. Advocating for yourself by being willing to shine a light on what's actually happening.

The more you do it, the easier it is. In all honesty, when I turned 30, it was like someone turned on the "Really??" switch in my brain. Assertiveness was suddenly second nature. Before then, it was much harder. I was much more concerned about being liked.

Here's something you can rely on. When you are a reasonable, decent person, you don't need to worry about offending people. If you accidentally do, just apologize. It happens. No big whoop.

<u>INTENTIONAL CRAZY</u>

This is an intentional and controlled use of erratic or strange behavior. Don't think it's a viable skill? Here's a newsflash:

an opponent relies on their target's behavior being
predictable.

**'Crazy' is unpredictable and very unattractive to
anyone who has mistakenly targeted you.**

⚠ TRUE STORY

*A student of mine, who survived being mugged and stabbed in an NY
subway, found herself in an elevator with a man who she knew was
dangerous one second after the doors closed. Without a second thought,
she held up her index finger and began to have a very tense and hushed
conversation with it, which eventually escalated into a knock-down, drag
out argument. With her finger.*

**When you know you are in mortal danger, you get to
act ANY WAY YOU NEED TO in order for your
opponent to lose interest.**

Pull out all the stops. There is no such concept as
embarrassment when it comes to saving your skin. Scream in
gibberish, howl like a wolf, develop a dramatic tick, drool
uncontrollably down your chin... nothing is out of bounds
when using your crazy skills. Be unpredictable! Be erratic!
Get weird and commit.

Even men use this tactic to avoid physical conflict.

⚠ TRUE STORY

My husband was about to get mugged at an ATM by four thugs that were waiting in their car for him to get his money. He was in a pickle: if he got his money, they would simply steal it from him and if he didn't get any money, they would intimidate him or possibly produce a weapon to get him to pull more money out of the ATM. He managed to find the only solution to eliminate both problems. When he saw them pull up directly behind him and stare him down, he cancelled his transaction. Then, he pretended that the ATM wouldn't accept his PIN and proceeded to whip up a nuclear meltdown rage that would have made Hugo Chavez take a step back. He acted so unstable, they wanted nothing to do with him. He walked right past them and they wouldn't even look at him.

With the exception of 'crazy' which gets used as needed, practicing these critical skills regularly will make them sharp and at the ready should you ever need to protect yourself. Be aware of your world all the time. Listen to your intuition. Be willing to assert yourself without hesitation and give powerful verbal resistance when your assertions go unheeded. And finally, consider putting your crazy hat on and don't take it off until it's safe.

UNDERSTANDING YOUR INSTINCTS

This chapter will explore your attitudes about hurting
another person physically, why defending yourself may not
be in your nature and how to overcome that resistance when
your life is at stake.

NATURE AND NURTURE

The two things that keep us safe and empowered also go
against our instincts and cultural conditioning.

Self defense is tricky for us because we have a deep instinct
to cooperate and get along with others. We are communal
creatures, hardwired to share, nurture and solve problems
through dialogue, not fists.

In the hunter/gather days, while the men were out hunting,
women of the tribe would venture out to collect water and
gather foods while tending to their children and the children
of their tribeswomen. Various incarnations of these roles still
exist in third world countries. It still takes a village. We are
gifted with verbal skills to resolve conflict. That's why we talk
so much. That's how we work it out.

It's against our nature to fight with our bodies. It's not that
we can't, it just that it's not our first instinct.

MIXED MESSAGES

We're so busy trying to fit into our youth and beauty obsessed culture, it's a wonder we have time think about anything else. The American media slathers us with messages that distract and separate us from our power.

You are exposed to a massive volume of disempowering messages everyday. When we watch TV or read magazines, we hang an IV bag of self-esteem poison; a noxious mixture of advertisements that slowly drips the fear of inadequacy into our veins, corroding us from the inside out. Our desire to be accepted and attractive is being siphoned, distilled and weaponized.

Society tells us we must be soft, sexy, slim and surrendered in order to be accepted. Don't be a bitch! You will die alone and miserable. In order to lead a happy life, pop culture tells us, we're allowed to have fat in two places: the left breast and the right breast. Never poop, fart or burp; very unattractive. Long, thick hair that smells like angels is a plus. Be smart, but not too smart. Be sassy, but know when to shut up. And you kinda get to say no, but you really shouldn't reject a man. Ever. Dress pretty, sit in the bar and let the men buy you judgement impairing beverages.

Welcome to the world according to the lowest, common denominator. Unfortunately, not only is the above paragraph reasonable to some men, they also believe the stripper likes them and the women in their favorite porn movies are genuinely enjoying themselves.

I'm not intimating that all men believe those things, but it's important to know that some absolutely do. It's a reality so make a space in your brain for this kind of ignorance and human miscalculation.

Constant pressure to be submissive combined with our cooperative nature can be a deadly cocktail.

One out of five women will tell you that this isn't working out so good. This will change when every woman decides to prioritize advocating for themselves all the time, everywhere. A shift happens every time a woman decides she's had enough and no longer cares what America thinks about her body, face, hair or clothes.

The statistics will drop when these empowered, aware women educate their daughters to think and stand up for themselves. When we teach our sons and daughters about respect by demonstrating respect. It will happen when we return to our most powerful strength, our native intelligence. Our intuitive guidance.

Women have the incredible ability to sense danger before it happens. We know damn well when something isn't quite right. We're just domesticated to the point that we talk ourselves out our own self preservation with wisdom-crushing social terrors such as, "I don't want to seem like a racist", "I don't want him to feel bad" etc.

WEAPON OF WILLINGNESS

Believe it or not, one of the biggest obstacles for women to overcome is not the strength or the power to fight for themselves, but the willingness to do so. You don't have to know *how to* physically defend yourself, you just have to be *willing*.

**120 seconds. That's how long the
average conflict lasts.**

Despite evidence to the contrary on our more insipid reality TV shows, most women don't like the idea of physically hurting someone. Even though it may make logical sense in terms of saving your own life, it's still unappealing and counterintuitive. For some, the willingness to hit, kick, bite or otherwise inflict injury upon another person is greater when the intent is to save oneself versus hurting another. It may sound crazy, but it's true.

Physically resisting someone doesn't require any fancy, complicated techniques, just basic human movement generally aimed at the vulnerable areas of your opponent. You must carry your willingness to defend yourself at all times. You are worth fighting for!

Your willingness to fight changes something in your vibe and makes you an unappealing target.

Staying off an opponent's radar is more important than knowing how to put someone in a wrist lock.

EYE OF THE TIGER

I am always amazed at the number of women in my seminars who balk at defending themselves, but wouldn't hesitate to defend a child. Any child, not even their own, even if they're not mothers. Why don't we feel the same ferocity about defending the ourselves?

If this sounds like you, then it's time that you split yourself in two: The gentle woman and the warrior who **protects** her.

Every woman has a warrior within, ready to be set loose. The sooner you connect with your warrior and give her permission to fight for you, the safer you'll be.

If you walk around with the eye of the tiger just beneath the surface and do whatever your intuition suggests, you may never need to physically defend yourself against an opponent.

Reminder: Opponents don't know who they're dealing with. They only know what you communicate with your attitude and body language.

Those who look for targets don't want a fight. They have instincts too and you can bet they are listening to theirs. Their intuition tells them who would quickly and easily surrender. A woman who carries herself with confidence doesn't look like an easy mark.

If you feel that learning self defense techniques will give you that confidence, then for the love of Pete, go learn them IMMEDIATELY. Skills can are handy, but how you carry yourself is more important. It's the look in your eye. It's okay if you have no idea how to physically defend yourself, just walk with the confidence of someone who does.

RESOLUTE RESOLUTION

Because of my mindset, awareness and willingness to heed my intuition, I have never been in a physical conflict outside of martial arts sparring. That said, I still decided that if someone attempted to assault me, I would have to assume they intended to kill me and I would not hesitate to do whatever I needed to in my own defense. I have no idea what that is and I'm not supposed to. It's making that decision *before* anything happens that matters.

Could you hurt or even kill someone who was trying to end your life?

Have you thought about what you would do? If you are so uncomfortable about this issue that you don't want to even think about it, it's particularly essential that you allow yourself to entertain these unsettling thoughts.

After reading through the physical resistance suggestions following this section, you have the opportunity to notice whether or not you are indeed squeamish about using your hands, fingers, knees, elbows and teeth as self defense tools.

Without the context of a life threatening physical conflict, the self defense techniques may seem barbaric but it is absolutely essential that you picture yourself successfully executing these techniques to make your escape.

Again, when you are going through it mentally *make sure* you end each scenario with your successful escape.

I don't mean to be cavalier. The thought of injuring or killing another human being, even in my own defense, makes me turn green. It's completely against my nature and it would haunt my conscience forever -- even if I was 100% justified.

In an effort to level the playing field you must allow yourself to see into the emotional darkness where dangerous people live.

It gives you a sort of empathy for them. Realize that the only thing that separates 'us' from 'them' is how we've processed the emotional trauma that every human being suffers at some point (broken hearts, betrayal, rejection, parental abuse etc). Some people cope, grow and move on. Some people hover in a holding pattern of arrested development. Some people snap, like brittle twigs, spending their lives perpetuating emotional pain and leaving a trail of survivors in the wake of their dysfunction.

And some people, for whatever reason, simply have no conscience. There are no rules, no acts of violent vulgarity that are outside of their comfort zone. They can act randomly or with forethought. We could be exactly the same if we too lost our sense of decency, empathy and conscience.

Each of us posses the potential to kill. We're all animals. Every human animal is born innocent and open. Through circumstance, genetic tendency, environmental conditioning and choice, certain behaviors are brought to the fore and cultivated into mastery. Some choices lead to the Dalai Lama and others created Hitler. Same babies, different circumstances.

The sooner you accept and illuminate your own shadow land, the safer you'll be. At the very least, you'll recognize it in others and won't fall into the trap of denial. Plus, once you've traipsed around your own darkness, it makes the darkness of others much less scary.

In a way, going there mentally and processing it emotionally keeps you from having to go there physically.

If you need to access your anger or rage to defend yourself, take some time to find out where that lives inside you so you can call upon it in an emergency. They're not called "Mad Skills" for nothing!

I believe that having even considered these scenarios is visible to the instincts of a dangerous person. You're not inviting a dark experience into your life, just acknowledging that this reality exists and then making a conscious choice to avoid it.

WELCOME TO YOUR PHYSICAL SKILLS

In this chapter you'll explore the physical self defense tools you were born with and come to understand that you currently possess the physical strength you would need to disable or seriously injure your opponent. You'll also learn how to form a simple plan in the moment.

YOU ARE WORTH FIGHTING FOR

When we see well trained martial artists or fighters, it's so tempting to think if only I knew all those skills, I would be safe. Being truly safe means not engaging in physical conflict in the first place.

**In reality it's not about what you can do,
it's about what your opponent *thinks* you can do.**

Physical conflict, although usually avoidable through awareness, intuition and verbal resistance, is a reality.

AGGRESSION EQUATION

Before you start putting your physical defense tools in your leather holster, it's important to understand how to apply them. No tool can serve it's purpose without a knowledgeable operator. Once you understand what your opponents need to make their plan happen, you can see how your skills can take away a crucial piece of their dubious puzzle.

Just like fire needs air, fuel (a combustible material) and an ignition source to burn, our opponents need some critical factors to be successful.

Key Elements in the Aggression Equation:

1. A target
2. Eyes to see their target
3. A short distance to their target (20 feet or less)
4. Hands to grab or use as weapons
5. Focus on their plan

A committed effort from you to take away one key element will most likely prevent your opponent's success.

You already have more than enough physical strength and power at your disposal to take away any one or all of these key elements. Here's where it gets emotionally tricky. I've never met a single women who didn't recoil at the idea of trying to pop out someone's eyes. Oh, I know... disgusting. Even more importantly, I would never want anyone to do it to me so hard to picture doing it to another person.

In that moment, our nature to nurture can cause us to hesitate, putting us at risk. Although our deep, abiding sense of 'do unto others' creates revulsion at the thought of going Mike Tyson on someone and biting their ear clean off, we must also realize that we would never act so threatening as to incite the same treatment against us.

When it comes to using your physical skills it's crucial to keep the compassionate angle: you are kicking/hitting/biting because you *love* yourself, not because you *hate that person*. You're just giving appropriate feedback, it's nothing personal.

WHAT YOU CAN DO RIGHT NOW

When it comes to successfully defending yourself physically, it takes way less than you may think. The puffer fish is a perfect example of what I'm talking about. This is a relatively small fish, barely even 12" long. It's a very non-threatening looking fish to such a degree it's been nicknamed the Hamster of the Sea.

But this cute little fish has one of the most effective defensive adaptions on the planet. If a shark approaches and attempts to eat the puffer fish, it blows up into a ballon. A ballon covered in razor-sharp spikes transforming the aqua-hamster into the Hellraiser Pin Head of the sea. The shark, realizing it has the fish equivalent of a thorny pinecone in it's mouth, spits out the puffer fish.

You just have to be willing to throw your spikes long enough, about 120 seconds, to let someone know that trying to eat you will turn out badly for them.

We must provide appropriate negative feedback towards *any* person who is acting like an out of control animal. The greater the threat, the more drastic the physical resistance may need to be.

Important Points To Consider:

1. Everything I recommend is *non-lethal and removes one or multiple key elements in the aggression equation. Having an opening for escape assumes you would run to safety, which eliminates the distance element.
2. All of the strike zones I recommend are areas that cannot be strengthened. No matter how big and strong your opponent may appear, there are places on his body that will always be sensitive and vulnerable.
3. No matter what physical strategy your opponent uses, every aggressive move on his part creates an opening for a counter strike on your part. <u>Always</u>.
4. Combine the suggestions below with loud, repeated verbal resistance. Yell NO! or FIRE! Yelling at your opponent can help you stay in the moment and stick with your plan. Believe it.

<u>TECHNIQUES THAT NEED NO PRACTICE, JUST YOUR WILLINGNESS</u>

YOUR TOOLS: Your **hands** are great tools. Either as a "lady fist" or the "beak".

The lady fist is made with your thumb on the outside pressed against your index finger knuckle. It's great for long fingernails since it doesn't require your fingers be completely curled up into your palm like a standard fist. The lady fist is deployed using the pinky side of the fist hitting the target, like a hammer. Try hitting it into your palm to feel the power of your awesome lady fist.

The beak is made by joining all of your fingers and thumb in a single point. Squeeze them together to make them a stronger. Try hitting your palm with the beak. Hit it hard to fully understand the potential of this tool. Doesn't take much, does it?

Your **elbows** are a great, pointy tool that can be deployed is someone is behind you. Alternately driving them back as hard as you can. You can easily knock the wind out of someone with the business end of your elbow.

Your **feet** are excellent for stomping, kicking and running to safety.

From the ground, your **legs** and feet become kick springs, keeping your opponent at bay.

Another tool is your **position**. Become dead weight and drop to the ground. It is much harder to drag someone who is dead weight on the ground. Especially if you can't get near them because they're kicking at you like a banshee. Men have the advantage when standing. Women have the advantage on the ground because our hips and legs are our most powerful body parts and serve as excellent self defense tools when deployed at ground level.

YOUR OPPONENT'S VULNERABILITIES

EYES: Taking away your opponent's sight is actually a classic primate strategy. Either poke them with extended fingers, strike with your lady fist or make the beak and strike at the eyes until you can escape. If your opponent is close, you are face to face and have even one hand free, put your thumb in the inner corner of his eye and push in. You both know what can happen next and most likely they'll decide it's not worth it. Commit to the icky.

NOSE: Hitting his nose as hard as you can with any part of your hand, open or closed, generally causes tearing, seeing stars and temporary loss of vision. Hitting with heel of your hand or the lady fist delivers the most power. The upper lip is also very sensitive and lips break and bleed causing a redirection of your opponent's focus. As you are hitting the strike zone(s) as hard as you can, keep hitting and yelling until you can escape. Worst case scenario, if you have no hands available, consider using your hard skull to smack the nose. Aim the top portion of your forehead at their soft nose and give a big nod yes forward only (NOT back then forward). Just know that the top of the forehead is the hardest part of the face so if you miss and accidentally hit theirs, it will hurt.

THROAT: The throat is another completely vulnerable place that cannot be strengthened. A solid strike of any kind to the adam's apple may cause a laryngospasm which will temporarily hinder his ability to breath. *This tactic can cause more severe damage and possibly death if laryngeal irritation and swelling leads to closing down of the airway. If you choose this one, I want you to be informed of the potential longer term effects. It's effective and potentially fatal.

FEET: Planting a heel stomp in the smack-dab center of your opponent's foot can not only create intense pain but actually break the bone. If you're wearing heels, you may not be able to do this but piercing a shoe and skin is the next best thing. Stomp, stomp, repeat!

GROIN: Knee strikes, elbow strikes, grab and squeeze or lady fists into the groin can cause crippling pain and vomiting. If grabbing isn't an option for you (long nails) an open hand strike to the groin can be equally effective. Or let your lady hammer do it's work.

FACE & NECK: Elbows are excellent tools. Fold your arm in toward you and you have a great way to strike across the face, jaw, neck or whatever you can hit in close range. Strike as hard as you can in the money spots and don't stop until you can get away or your opponent runs.

HANDS: Don't bother trying to peel a strong hand off you by the thumb. The thumb is the strongest digit on the hand.

The pinky is the weakest. If at any point you can grab a pinky finger, hold it tight with your whole hand and yank fast and hard in the opposite direction (toward the back of the hand). It's easier to break a pinky than a pencil. You just have to really go for it.

KNEES: Take away your opponent's base (and therefore, his ability to generate force from his legs) and it's over. Although strong muscles attach above and below, the knee joint itself is vulnerable to movement in the wrong direction. Kick at your opponents knee, preferably back towards them or to either side and you can snap the ligaments that hold the knee in place. Chop them down like a tree. The bigger they are...

FLESH: Guess what your strongest muscle is? Your jaw, naturally! You can generate an incredible bite force. If your hands are occupied, bite whatever you can sink your teeth into.

All of the above tactics disrupt an element of the aggression equation. Think puffer fish. Put up your spikes just long enough to create your escape.

PLAN TO BE SUCCESSFUL

Part of a successful offense is having a plan. One of the biggest disadvantages of being confronted suddenly by a dangerous person is women get overwhelmed and freeze. Being a firefighter taught me something really important. People used to ask me, "Weren't you scared to go running

INTO a burning building?" The answer was always that I was so focused on my job, so task oriented, that going in was the *only* thing I thought about. Being cautious and aware was one of our tasks. We were always aware of the signs of trouble so we could prevent ourselves getting trapped or caught in a deadly flashover.

Once you have taken the time to really think about how you would handle certain encounters, then you have a rough pre-plan.

Granted, things rarely go according to plan, but having a plan, even if it's just a rough idea of what you would do, is totally key. Realize that someone who means to do you harm already has a plan. They are very focused on it.

When you have a plan, you have choices; you are not trapped. You can put your focus on executing the plan and that vibe will be felt by anyone who is sizing you up.

MAKING A PLAN

Example: A strange man steps into the elevator with you. As he walks in, check in with your survival instincts. *You* size *him* up. It's a split second of intuitive inquisition that will tell you if you need to step out.

If the doors close and only then does it become clear that this person is dangerous, start thinking about which vulnerable areas you are most comfortable striking. The eyes? Nose? Maybe you prefer to use your strong legs to deliver a knee to the groin? Or stomp his foot? Is he wearing a tie that you could possibly yank to control his position? Are his pants below his butt making it harder for him to take big strides? Where are his knees? Do you have a heavy purse your could hit him with?

These thoughts, as unsavory as they are, change your energy (and the weather) instantly. By the way, do you know where the alarm button is? Many modern elevators are monitored by security personnel.

Worrying about what he is going to do to you smells like fear and weakness. Thinking about what you would do to him smells like power.

Start planning your escape before a single thing has happened. This shifts the energy in your favor. If he wants to hurt you, he's counting on two things: surprising an unsuspecting person and fear making them weak and compliant. If you are strategizing the best way to incapacitate him, you've already identified him as dangerous; his cover is blown and you clearly aren't going to just fold like a cheap card table.

This is all communicated non-verbally. You changed from target to empowered just by making a plan and standing next to him like someone who will unleash a flurry of physical and verbal resistance if he takes one step toward you. To a fly on the wall, a man walked into an elevator with a woman. But energetically, there is so much communication flying around that space you could cut it with a knife. That's how animals assess each other.

You carry blankets and a flashlight in your car in case of a road emergency. You have a weeks' worth of food in your pantry in case of a weather emergency. Make a self defense plan by remembering the list of vulnerable body areas you can confidently strike and practice mentally in case of a personal safety emergency.

A WORD ABOUT MONKEYS

Aggressive male behavior directed towards females is not limited to humans. Our primate ancestors have their version this cultural phenomenon. Except in the primate world, it's handled very differently. Biological Anthropologist Dr Newton-Fisher of the University of Kent, studied a particular community of East African chimpanzees in Budongo Forest, Uganda.

He observed that the females were often subject to severe aggression by the older adult males. He also observed females engage in cooperative retaliation. After a female had been abused by a male, a group of two to six female members of the community would retaliate with vocalizations, threatening gestures and sometimes physically fighting the male responsible for the aggression.

The abused females solicited support from other females; they formed a monkey posse to shout down or beat up the guilty male. Those female chimps really know how to take their natural affinity for cooperation and make it fierce. That's some sweet monkey justice.

MENTAL TRAINING: MIND-BODY CONNECTION

This chapter will explain the fundamentals of mental training and briefly explore the mind-body connection of self defense.

ASSAULT PSYCHOBIOLOGY

It should be noted that for many women who have survived an attempted or completed assault, that trauma can create a significant and lasting impact on their emotional and physical well being. According to [13]Burgess and Hazelwood (2001), the majority of survivors shared one common emotion after their trauma: Fear. Not shame, anger nor humiliation. They felt the number one fear of women in general, which is to be killed by a man. Despite what happened to them, they felt lucky to have survived.

One out of five women, depending on their trauma, may develop Post Traumatic Stress Disorder as well as a multitude of phobias and neurotic tendencies. Their confidence crushed, they may be too overwhelmed to resume regular activities for weeks or months. If the survivor decides to press charges, she will most likely have to relive her intimate trauma in a public setting, in the presence of her

---

[13] Hazelwood, Robert, R., Burgess, Ann W. Practical Aspects of Rape Investigation A Multidisciplinary Approach (Third Edition). Boca Raton: CRC Press, 2001

abuser and be subjected to character assassination by the defense attorney.

Without swift and effective intervention, this emotional burden can take it's toll on the body. When we have too much stress or an event disrupts our ability to turn our stress coping mechanisms off, the effects can weaken our immune systems and literally shrink parts of our brains. A woman in who is in an active state of traumatization is not a good candidate for mental training as it may be overwhelming. She will most likely not be able to empower herself until she has begun to heal from her past experience, which takes time, lots of support from friends and family and a good therapist.

Some women become obsessed with their trauma, turning inward, becoming ill, never recovering nor returning to their former lives. Others are able to move on and live their lives but the event still remains in their psyche. Even years after an assault, women may still get triggered and sent straight back to their terrifying memories.

Although the wounds of rape can heal and fade, they will always be there. The only thing that changes is the dialogue about the experience.

That said, how we choose to change and grow from traumatic events can help us cope with future stress and make us stronger.

MIND-BODY BOND

You need to be prepared for what your body will do in an emergency so you can layer that into your mental training. When we practice self defense scenarios in our minds, it's always done in a safe place where we are secure and calm. When confronted with the terrifying reality of an opponent surprising you in the shadows, you will have to deal with an adrenalin response.

When your survival center (limbic system) assesses your life is being threatened, your sympathetic nervous system (fight or flight) is activated and your adrenal glands will pump out enough adrenalin to raise the dead. If you are not aware that your body will do this, it can be very discombobulating and contribute to the compulsion to freeze.

Here's what you can expect from an adrenalin rush:
- *Tunnel vision*: Your pupils will dilate to allow in maximum light, which limits peripheral vision and creates tunnel vision.
- *Racing heartbeat*: Adrenalin is a hormone called epinephrine which tells your heart to beat faster and it raises your blood pressure.
- *Time slows down*: Everything inside of you is moving at warp nine so the outside world seems to move at a dream-like crawl.
- *You are stronger and faster:* Blood is diverted from your organs into your limbs temporarily so you can fight or flee. This might also cause nausea.

- *You can't think clearly:* Blood is also diverted from parts of your brain which makes problem solving difficult.
- *Decreased coordination*: Once some parts of your brain have less blood, it will make it more difficult for your muscles and nervous system to communicate.

Not so much fun. Just processing all that adrenalin is hard enough; having to do it while saving yourself is a huge challenge. The more focused you can be on your plan or strategy that you have been mentally practicing, the more effective you will be at coming to your own rescue.

Soldiers, police officers and other dangerous jobs require calm and steely focus during life threatening situations. They can't afford to have an adrenalin response distracting them from their work. Know how they get over it? By being in actual life threatening environments again and again and again. No matter how much training they receive, it takes actually functioning during dangerous, high-tension scenarios to control this natural response. Since the whole point of Unbreakable Woman is to avoid one of these scenarios, be aware that it may happen and continually practice your mental training.

⚠ TRUE STORY

While I was working as a firefighter, I got a def-con one bladder infection. While in the hospital, I received Cipro for the first time. Cipro is the Sherman tank of antibiotics, it will kill anything. Turns out I was deadly allergic to it. I remember trying to stay calm as my lungs and throat began to swell shut. I was literally at the edge of death, turning blue, too tired to cough any longer, when they slammed adrenalin (epinephrin) into my IV. I sat bolt upright and yelled at the top of my lungs as my heart beat out of my chest. The "epi rush" was far more terrifying than my inability to breathe. I was sure I would have a heart attack. Afterward, I felt like I had run a marathon. Adrenalin is a trip.

GO THERE MENTALLY

As mentioned throughout this book, mental training is your opportunity to imagine a self defense scenario from beginning to end with you successfully escaping. Be sure to spend extra time with the situations you find the most scary so you can desensitize yourself. There are many reasons for this mental practice:

1. When you have imagined every possible scenario, it will be much harder for a criminal to surprise you, which is often a key element in their plan.
2. Once you've pictured the threat and your response with a successful outcome, it reduces your fear of the situation, increases your confidence and makes you a less likely target.
3. The practice of mental training will help you develop consistent strategies that can become second nature. When faced with a possible threat, you will already have a very good idea of what to do. You'll be so busy focusing on your tactics in the moment that you won't have time to think about your fear.

An example of mental training:

I discover that I am out of milk at 10:30 p.m. I don't have a car, and the only store within walking distance is a convenience store that's in a sketchy part of my neighborhood.

Before anything else, I must ask myself, just because I *want* the milk for breakfast, do I *need* the milk for breakfast? Is it worth putting my life at risk? Is there anything else in the house I can eat for breakfast? Can I turn this into a positive situation, and in the morning, treat myself to breakfast at my favorite diner? We often get so focused on our immediate desires, we forget to put them in perspective.

If I decide that I absolutely must go to that store, by myself, I will mentally train as I go.

a. I take the purse with the long strap so I can put it across my chest and keep my hands free. As I walk to the store, I'm glancing around. I walk as far from blind corners, alleys and tall bushes as I can. If someone jumps out at me, I will scream NO! and pound at their face with my fists until I can get away. I'll run to the house where I can see a family watching television through their window and call 9-1-1.

b. On the way home, if someone seems to be following me, I will cross the road to see if they do also, confirming my suspicions. I will call 9-1-1 and let them know my location and that a suspicious person is following me and ask them for instructions. I could also look for a public place to step into along the way to lose my potential opponent.

c. If I fail to notice that someone is following me until the person has grabbed me from behind, first I'll drop whatever I'm holding to free up my hands. If his arm is around my neck like a choke hold, I'll grab his arm with both hands and pull it down away from my windpipe and start screaming 'FIRE!; I'll stomp his feet and bite his arm as hard as I can as I drop to the ground. If he comes to the ground with me, I'll kick down at him with my heel yelling 'FIRE' and if he's standing I'll kick at up at him to keep him away, etc.

Reminder: To stay in your power, always be thinking about what *you're going to do*.

Picture your daily routine, your house and your habits. Are there areas where you are unintentionally creating opportunities for a criminal to gain easy access to you? (ie: you live in an apartment building and you leave your door unlocked when you go to the laundry room). This awareness is a great gift and hopefully leads you to amend your habits to make it as difficult as possible for anyone to harm you.

Every time you get on a plane, there's a little bit of mental training going on. The flight crew shows you where your exits are in case of an emergency. In life, you need to be your own flight crew. Always casually noticing your exits, the people and the activities around you.

Use the scenarios in the next chapter to begin your mental training. Think about how you might handle yourself in a similar situation or avoid it altogether. Every personality is different so it's important that you imagine what strengths you can realistically bring to the equation to help yourself.

SECTION V - Test Your Knowledge

"I learned that courage was not the absence of fear, but the triumph over it. The brave man is not he who does not feel afraid, but he who conquers that fear." -Nelson Mandela

PRACTICE SCENARIOS 2.0

☞ Dissect real world situations

☞ Learn to see red flags

☞ Practice mental training

Now that you've learned some tools to help you stay in your power, the manipulation tactics that criminals use and how to connect to the arsenal of critical safety skills that you were born with, let's revisit the original scenarios through your new eyes.

Before you read the breakdowns below, consider going back to original scenarios and pick out as many red flags as you can. With each red flag, what action would you take to either prevent the scenario in the first place, compel the criminal to leave or remove yourself from the situation? There are many strategies that could work so it's not about finding "the" one. It's about practicing your mental training. Get in the habit of thinking your way through everyday situations that could devolve into dangerous scenarios and how to manifest a positive outcome with confidence and creativity.

These scenarios will allow you to practice:

1. SEEING where lack of awareness leaves someone more vulnerable to exploitation.
2. IDENTIFYING red flags that are generally consistent throughout each type of situation.
3. TRUSTING that when you get intuitive information and see these red flags that you are perceiving things correctly so you can act without hesitation.

Note: I suggest calling 9-1-1 throughout this book as a safety tactic. Many cities don't have a separate non-emergency number to report suspicious people and encourage the use of the emergency number. Other larger or higher-crime cities may have a different policy. Keep that in mind anytime I recommend the use of 9-1-1 and contact your local police precinct to find out the most appropriate option should you need it.

IN DETAIL: STRANGER DANGER

The Parking garage of your work place - Leah arrived at work on time but the garage was jammed. She had to park where there was space available and the spot wasn't very close to the elevator.

▷ *Knowing that parking garages are common places for criminals to operate, a safe move would be to go back at mid-day or when others are at lunch and move her car closer.*

Up against some deadlines, she works a little late and is one of the last people to leave.

▷ *If there is anyone else working, male or female, she could either wait for them or ask them to walk her to her car. If she is parked in a bad place or knows there aren't a lot of people around when she leaves, find someone trustworthy (security, janitorial etc) to walk her to her car. Leaving the car in a faraway location and not having an escort can open the door for an opportunist.*

Upon arriving in the garage, she notices a man loitering.

▷ *There are usually no good reasons for anyone to be loitering on the upper floors of a parking garage. This is legitimately suspicious on it's own. This is the first intuitive clue that something is not right.*

Unsettled, she turns and walks toward her car.

▷ *Her intuition gave her a ping which unsettled her. This is all the evidence she needs to avoid this lurker. The moment she became unsettled, she needed to turn right around and walk back. She ignored this important signal. As soon as she saw a random man lurking around the lot, that is reason enough to snap her fingers and say loud enough for him to hear, "Oops, forgot my keys..." get back in the elevator and get out of Dodge. She could also elect to get on her phone while acknowledging him. In this case, the cell phone is not a dangerous distraction but a life line to a witness.*

Luckily, her car is in the opposite direction. She feels like she needs to look over her shoulder but she doesn't want to appear nervous like she is watching him.

▷ *Her intuition is giving her more signals, but she continues to ignore them. She is worried about what this man thinks rather than letting him know she sees him and potentially his intentions. Not acknowledging him can give him the idea that she is intimidated and the potential element of surprise. She may be giving him a green light.*

She picks up the pace, hearing only the echoey clip-clop sound of her heels as she walks, thinking one thought: *get to the car.*

▷ *She believes that her safety will be guaranteed if she can only get to her car. She ignores that fact that the individual her intuition has deemed dangerous is nearby and she is more focused on her car than his whereabouts.*

As she arrives safely at her car, Leah reaches into her purse to get her keys, feeling relieved and a little silly. As she disarms the alarm and opens the door, she is suddenly shoved hard from behind...

▷ *She didn't have the keys out prior to getting to her car making her have to stop and rummage through her purse, putting her attention on finding the keys rather than her surroundings. She never cleared (checked) her immediate vicinity before creating access to her car by unlocking it. She never looked in her car to confirm that no one was waiting inside (a good habit). She didn't think to look into the windows of the car (for reflections) to verify that no one was behind her. At night, in a lit area, car windows are as good as mirrors.*

SUMMARY: The moment she "noticed" the man loitering, that should have been her cue to either acknowledge him and decide whether continuing to her car is a good idea, create a witness with a phone call or exit. By the time the second signal came, that should have been the point that she abandoned her plan to walk to her car and return to her building. Another option would have been to call 9-1-1 then and there to report the suspicious person, then find someone trustworthy to escort her to her car. By staying focused on getting to her car and purposefully ignoring the creepy man, she was more worried about what he would do or think instead of what she could do to stay safe. This opened the door to danger.

SCENARIO PREVENTION: By arriving to work a little early for a safer parking spot or asking someone to walk her to her car she could have avoided this scenario.

RELATIVE TO YOU: Granted every scenario will vary, but another reliable tactic is to acknowledge the person you're concerned about in a very casual way. "Hey. How's it goin'." This is not about being friendly, it's about communicating the intention 'I've got my eye on you.' This lets them know you see them, you're not afraid of them and eliminates the possibility of surprise. Even if you are afraid, stow it. Remember, strangers only know what you tell them about you with your body language and vibe. At that moment, as far as he's concerned you are armed and dangerous. You'll have plenty of time to freak out once you're safely home.

Mall or grocery store parking lot/putting things in the car/trunk - In the middle of the afternoon Donna is walking to her car with a cart overflowing with grocery bags, dog food, 24 packs of water etc.

▷ Parking lots are a common place for criminals to vet targets. At just about every grocery store, after they bag the items they ask if you need help out. Her answer needed to be yes.

This is just the first of many errands she needs to run and she is behind schedule. She realizes she will be late to pick up her kids from their play date so she calls to let the parents know. She pops the trunk and starts to put bags in.

▷ She is in a hurry and very distracted. She is completely unaware of what and who are around her when she pops her trunk, creates access to her car and proceeds to pack her car with her back to the world.

A man appears abruptly, surprising her. "Oh, I'm sorry" he says. "My goodness, I didn't mean to scare you."

▷ If he truly intended to not startle her, he would have announced his presence verbally first with, "Excuse me..." or something similar. This makes him is a little too apologetic and insincere. Red flag number one.

She catches her breath and despite feeling uneasy, she tells him it's fine.

▷ The moment that stranger made her feel uneasy was her cue to stop and pay attention to what was happening in front of her. That was her intuition recognizing and reporting that something about him was not right. Various strategies could have been used to get him to go away and that's when it needed to happen first.

"Let me help you with those." he offers. "No thank you. I can manage." she replies. "Well, aren't you the model of a modern women. Please, I insist. Happy to lend a hand to a damsel in distress."

▷ First, she said no and he ignores her which shows a lack of respect for her right to refuse him and to have her own boundaries. Then

his compliments are so condescending he actually tips his hand by inadvertently exposing his true feelings about women. He is trying to put her in a submissive role where he is more powerful. The great irony is he has positioned himself as coming to her "rescue". Red flags everywhere.

Although a little put off by his creepy comments, she doesn't want to get into it with him so she continues putting bags in the trunk, leaning in to keep them organized since there are so many to load, "That's okay. I'm in a rush."

⊳ *Another message from her intuition has been ignored in the name of wanting to get to her next appointment. Instead of stopping, slamming the trunk shut and telling him to go away or she'll call the police, she lightly rebuffs him and continues to turn her back to him.*

He looks at her disapprovingly and says, "It doesn't make you less independent if you let someone help you."

⊳ *This is a tactic change. He's gone from her knight in shining armor to a snarky judge of character. A manipulation designed to get her to try to change her behavior to get approval from him.*

He notices the family stickers on her rear window, depicting a man, woman, two girls, a boy and a dog. "I'll bet your kids keep you jumping." He laughs a little and looks at his watch. "I'll bet it's just about time to pick someone up from school. C'mon, four hands are quicker than two, let's get you on your way."

⊳ *Another tactic change. Still ignoring her refusals, he used visible information to make some assumptions and employed a familiar tone, that is inappropriate for a stranger, to get her to comply. He is trying to make himself seem familiar to her and using 'let's' to help insinuate himself into her current plan as if he is on her side and they can work as a team.*

She considers the heavier items in her cart and reluctantly agrees. She pulls her keys from her purse and unlocks all of the doors. Instantly, his expression changes and he lunges at her...

SUMMARY - Her personal safety risk stemmed from a laser like focus on her task list for the day. Her unwillingness to detach from her schedule distracted her and disconnected her from the vital intuitive information she continued to receive while in the presence of this stranger. From the moment her intuition told her beware that man, she needed to abandon her plan to get on the road as soon as possible. She needed to take care of the situation unfolding in front of her by telling him to leave her alone and make a big scene. Everything after that was simply further proof that he was attempting to get compliance from her for whatever dubious reason.

SCENARIO PREVENTION: If she had asked someone from the store to help her, this scenario could have been avoided.

RELATIVE TO YOU: Always give yourself permission to reject any offer from a stranger, male or female. Some may be genuine and others may be sketchy to dangerous. If a stranger triggers an intuitive ping, that may mean you are in the presence of an unstable person. You have no other way of knowing a stranger's intentions so err on the side of caution. Who cares what a stranger thinks of you? Also, in a situation where your life is in danger, don't forget to abandon your attachment to your purchases -- those can be repurchased. In many cases where shoppers are attacked outside of stores, they struggle with their opponents and don't let go of their bags! Leave everything behind and get yourself to safety whether it be in your locked car or back into the store.

Walking or jogging through a secluded path - Beth is an avid outdoor jogger and loves to explore new places. She downloaded some great new music, charged up her iPod, drove to a new path and after a few warm up stretches, she begins her route.

▷ *She decided to venture onto an unknown trail by herself.*

It's beautiful weather and the path is in bloom with flowers, buzzing bees and dense green leaves on all the trees. Her favorite song comes on so she pumps up the volume.

▷ *She eliminated one of her senses and it disabled her ability to properly take in what was happening around her.*

She notices a man lying on a bench just off this trail. Although lying down, his eyes are open and he's not sleeping. He's dressed a little warm for the weather and looks like he just came off a construction site. Although this seems strange to her, it's a nice day to relax outside so she doesn't think much about it and jogs right on by, focused on the path.

▷ *Her noticing that his eyes are open is the first sign of potential trouble. She was given a lot of intuitive information very fast which is significant but she ignores it or doesn't recognize the importance. She doesn't acknowledge him, which opens the possibility that, in his mind, he is unseen by her.*

As she heads down a narrow section of the path, surrounded on either side by dense forest, she senses that there is another runner right behind her and they are trying to get past. She glances over her shoulder to motion for them to pass and she notices that the runner is wearing jeans, work boots and a heavy flannel shirt.

▷ *She just spotted that stranger behind her in obvious pursuit. Drastic measures need to be taken (verbal and physical resistance) without hesitation to escape this safety emergency.*

This "runner" suddenly lurches forward, wrapping his arms around her, tackling her to the ground...

SUMMARY: *Running on an unfamiliar, heavily wooded trail, alone and disabling her sense of hearing are personal safety risks. Then, she ignored all of the intuitive data that came flooding into her consciousness, not realizing it held critical information that would impact her personal safety. If her ears were free to hear, she may have heard his footfalls long before he got too close.*

SCENARIO PREVENTION: *If she had a running partner or a medium to large dog, this scenario could have been avoided.*

RELATIVE TO YOU: *The opportunistic criminal is looking for a single, easy take down and thick brush to provide coverage to hide his crime. Knowing this, some steps can be taken to vastly reduce the likelihood of it happening to you. Have a running partner, keep your ears open to your surroundings and scope out trails with your partner or a decent size dog prior to the run. Criminals don't like dogs because they can't predict their behavior and it's too much of a risk. Carrying mace could be helpful, but realize any weapon you carry could be used against you.*

In a perfect world, you should be able to run alone, anywhere at anytime with your music as loud as you like. Unfortunately, we don't live in a perfect world. If you can't run with a partner or with a dog, consider a well populated running path or go to a nearby school track or gym.

Getting lost in an unfamiliar city - It's just starting to get dark and Lori is searching for the great new bar her friends texted her about 30 minutes ago. They are already two drinks into happy hour and want her to join them. Using the address in the text, her GPS led her to an unfamiliar part of town but her friends raved about the cheap, signature cocktails so it would make sense that it was a hole in the wall in a sketchy area. The only parking space close to the address appears to be an abandoned parking lot. It doesn't feel right, but the GPS told her it was here so she gets out and walks around looking for the bar.

▷ *This place already feels off. Instead of trusting her gut, she trusts the GPS and a text from her friend who has been drinking.*

Lori can't find the bar or the address. She walks around for a good five minutes more, seeing only run down apartment buildings and a few store fronts. Finally, it dawns on her that her friends must have gotten the address wrong and she is in a bad neighborhood. She starts to get nervous and quickly turns tail to head back to her car. While walking, she tries to call her friends but her battery is out of juice.

▷ *By continuing to look for the address, she allowed herself to get deep enough into the neighborhood that she started to get nervous, which can attract a criminal element looking to escalate and exploit her fear. Not keeping her phone charged eliminated an important safety tool. She needed to calmly and casually walk back to her car.*

A wave of panic comes over her. She passes a busy laundromat when she notices a couple of guys are walking toward her on her side the sidewalk. She knows they are trouble.

▷ *Panic is very disabling. The most important thing she could have done was to take a deep breath, stay calm and assess her best plan of action. When her intuition pings her twice, first with 'noticing' then with 'knowing' the two guys were trouble, she has access to a public place with people inside but she doesn't seek shelter there. There are plenty of honest, good people in "bad neighborhoods" who are willing to help. Even if the laundromat patrons do nothing, their very presence might deter her potential opponents.*

She hugs her purse tightly to her side, looks down and walks as quickly as she can, hoping they will ignore her.

▷ *Putting her head down and ignoring the two guys communicates fear with body language. It tells them that they have already intimidated her and she will probably fold like a cheap card table. She is giving them a green light.*

As she approaches them, one of them steps in front of her and says, "Hey, do you have a cigarette?", she stops and says no. He says, "How about some change. You got any change?" as his friend walks around and steps behind her...

▷ *Her actions will very much depend on the threat. If they just want to rob her, then she needs to calmly offer her purse, go to the laundromat and call 9-1-1. If they intend to be violent, she needs to scream 'fire!' or act like a crazy person but somehow make huge scene to appear to be more trouble than she's worth.*

SUMMARY: *Her first big mistake was parking and venturing out on foot, at night, in an unfamiliar area, by herself. When looking for an unfamiliar place, get a visual lock on your destination address*

BEFORE looking for parking. Not having a working cell phone adds stress to her mounting nervousness. Although she couldn't make an actual call, she could have received or made a fake phone call, creating a witness to anyone watching. By the time she realizes she's somewhere she shouldn't be, instead of choosing to calm herself down and talk herself through a plan, she panics. Her panic prevents her from seeing an obvious escape, the laundromat. Now she has to deal with these thugs which may require physical resistance.

SCENARIO PREVENTION: If she had stayed in her car and driven to a safe place (gas station etc) to confirm the address and reassess the plan, this scenario could have been avoided.

RELATIVE TO YOU: If your friends invite you to a great new place that appears to be in a bad neighborhood, don't go by yourself. If you can't find anyone to go with you, meet them afterward in a familiar location. It is very common for a GPS to send drivers to wrong places. Trust your instincts and always keep your phone charged. It could be your lifeline.

Repair/delivery men and contractors - Nicole is showering when the water turns ice cold. Covered in goosebumps, she towels up and heads to the basement. After monkeying with her hot water heater which is probably from the Kennedy administration, she knows she has to call a repair professional. She can't afford to replace it so she goes online searching for a company promising the cheapest, quickest service. After deciding on a company that boasts "local contractors at your door in minutes!", she makes the call and gets dressed.

As advertised, there's a knock on the door 20 minutes later. Hair still wet, she answers. A burly, late 30-something repair man dressed in sloppy 'work blues' with a paint splattered tool box that looks older than the water heater, waits to be invited in. He looks Nicole up and down and says, "You look like you were just in a hot shower." Repair man humor? Maybe, but it instantly creeps her out. She hesitates for a moment, he definitely gives her the willies, but she doesn't want to seem rude.

▷ *This slovenly repair man is taking social liberties that she has not granted him. He looks unprofessional and has just confirmed that his conduct is also unprofessional. All of this pinged her intuition with the 'creepy' message. Her instincts tell her he's trouble, but she ignores them for the sake of being nice.*

"I can't fix the problem from here." he says, not joking. She takes an instant disliking to him, but figures it's more important that he be better at fixing water heaters than making conversation.

▷ *More intuitive data about this stranger. She decides to ignore her intuition and his rudeness for the sake of expediting the repair of her water heater.*

Nicole leads him straight to the basement.

▷ *Although it didn't result in anything, it is never a good idea to turn your back on a stranger and lead them into a basement or any room for that matter. Show them where to go and invite them to lead the way. Stay between the stranger and the exit.*

After she answers a few basic questions and he starts to work, he looks her up and down again. "Your husband is a lucky man." Uncomfortable and feeling the need to appear confident, she says she's not married but has a boyfriend. "Well, he's got his hands full with you, I can tell ya that. Why don't you go get him so I can explain the problem with this." She smiles weakly, says he's out with friends. Feeling unsettled, she excuses herself and says she'll be back down in a few minutes.

▷ *It's completely inappropriate for any contractor or repair person to make these types of personal comments. His "compliment" makes her uncomfortable which is a sign of trouble, but she doesn't address it. Instead, she shares truthful, personal information with him and fuels the fire for more inappropriate behavior. His second comment shows not only that he clearly has no respect for women but that he might also be trying to figure out if they are alone in the house. Her desire to 'appear confident' is her intuition giving her more information. Why should she care if this man thinks she is confident? Because she is afraid of him and wants to prove to him (and possibly herself) that she isn't. That proving could also be denial about how dangerous this stranger actually is, particularly since she has already granted him access to her.*

Upstairs in the bathroom, she is drying her hair. She bends down to put the dryer away and when she looks in the mirror, she sees him standing behind her. Startled, she spins around to face him, heart beating out of her chest. "Oops. Didn't mean to sneak up on you like that."

▷ *His apology is a misdirection to help her rationalize away her instincts. Anyone who doesn't want to startle someone generally announces their presence verbally to prevent surprise. Especially when in someone else's home. Also, it is unprofessional and inappropriate to wander into areas of her home where he hasn't been given specific permission to enter. Taking these kind of liberties speaks volumes about the intent of a person. This behavior in and of itself is enough to constitute a strong verbal resistance response.*

She regains her composure. Not wanting to appear afraid, she casually asks, "Are you through already? Can you show me what you did?" Nicole tries to leave the bathroom, but he stands at the door, blocking her...

SUMMARY:

Nicole made a serious mistake before the contractor arrived at her door. She searched blindly on the Internet instead of calling a friend for a referral or doing 5 minutes of research. The moment Nicole got her first intuitive ping that this man was trouble was the beginning of the end. As his inappropriate behavior continued to create an intuitive response upping her anxiety, she balked at every opportunity to tell him to leave until it was too late. When he was asking for her husband, she could have shut that angle down by saying what was happening in the moment, "I know you think you are being complimentary but it's inappropriate and it makes me uncomfortable. I would appreciate it if you would just fix the problem as quickly as possible and be on your way." Maybe follow up with the threat of calling his boss and complaining.

By drying her hair with a blowdryer, she eliminated any warning that the plumber was coming up the stairs. Although they were both aware that his behavior and intentions were intimidating and creating fear for her, she was in denial which led to her putting herself in a compromising position.

SCENARIO PREVENTION: If she had refused to let him in and sent him away, this scenario could have been avoided.

<u>RELATIVE TO YOU</u>: *If a contractor shows up and makes you uncomfortable, get another contractor. Just because you need help doesn't mean you have to accept help from the first person that shows up at your door, even if you called them. Get a read on them before you let them in and if anything feels off, make an excuse, tell them your spouse/partner already called a friend to fix it and apologize for wasting their time, say whatever you need to in order to shoo them away. You can expect that the person on the receiving end of this rejection may not appreciate it and may have some choice things to say about you. Who cares. You're not rude, you're smart. No creepy strangers get to come in your house. Period.*

In the old days, it took some financial commitment to place an ad in the phone book. These days, anyone can get a pseudo business name listed on the Internet. Start with trusted websites like Angie's List or Yelp. Read the reviews and match the website address and phone numbers you call to the ones listed on these platforms. It is best to have a list of trusted contractors (plumbing, electrical, heating/air conditioning, locksmith, etc.) before you need to call them.

IN DETAIL: ACQUAINTANCE DANGER

Co-workers - Jessica has been working with Mike for about 7 months. They get along and work well on projects. Lately, he's been teasing about asking her out. It was cute at first, but its become a little annoying. She has no desire to have a workplace romance with him or anyone else, but wants to prevent any awkward tension between them. So every time he "jokes" about it, she always laughs and redirects him gently.

▷ *This is such a tricky situation. She is smart to keep it the energy casual when rebuffing him, but her mistake is that she is not direct enough with her intentions. If he is fishing to see if she's possibly interested, her responses continue to leave the door open. Perhaps this is why he persists. If she casually let him know, in no uncertain terms, that she is not interested in a relationship with him, it would accomplish two things: prevent future overtures and reveal the content of his character if he continues to pursue her. If he ignores her clear rejection, that shines a light on his intentions and changes the dynamic from playful banter to sexual harassment.*

Finally, he actually does invite her out for an after work drink. He seems like a nice enough guy, other people seem to like him and it could reinforce their teamwork dynamic. Plus, colleagues often socialize after work so she decides to go.

▷ *Instead of seeing this development as contrary to her choice to avoid workplace relationships, as her intuition is telling her, she is trying to rationalize why it might be an okay idea. This is a critical moment where her acceptance of his offer needs to be followed up with a clear exchange of his intentions, her intentions, boundaries and perhaps even some ground rules if needed.*

Mike shows up in her office a couple of hours before they're supposed to leave and offers to drive, adding that it would be easy to drop her at her car afterwards.

▷ *This is definitely a potential red flag. By allowing him to drive, she is relying on him. He has the keys and the power to dictate when and where they go. If he is unscrupulous, this could be a dangerous choice on her part.*

Always looking for ways to reduce her carbon footprint, she agrees. At the bar, the waitress serves them both a couple of rounds and Jessica is really enjoying a lively conversation.

Then, Mike makes a blatant sexual advance. Although she never says 'no' directly, she very gently and politely declines.

▷ *He makes a move because she has never said a definitive 'no' to him and in perhaps in his mind, she is leading him on. Her unwillingness to be direct and say exactly what she means leaves room for interpretation and confusion.*

It's getting late and she hints that she's ready to go but he wants to hang out a little longer. He says, "Just one more drink. C'mon, it's the least you could do after shooting me down." he adds playfully. Despite his levity, a wave of anxiety passes over her, but she doesn't want to cause tension at work tomorrow, so she agrees. Suddenly impatient, he goes to bar for the last round of drinks.

▷ *This is another red flag. She can't see the drink being made and has no guarantee that it is safe for her to consume.*

Jessica wakes up in her car, disoriented, dizzy and nauseous at 4:37am...

SUMMARY: *From the moment he began "joking" with her, she needed to shut the door on his perception that she was a possible conquest. A clear conversation about her desire to not have a relationship would have resolved any confusion he might have had and help reveal her co-workers intentions. If he continued to pursue her, she needed to tell him that it was unwanted, making her uncomfortable and request that he discontinue his overtures. At the point where he continued to ignore her requests to stop, a manager and human resources should be notified. Sometimes, all it takes is attendance of a sexual harassment seminar to reset the man's understanding of what acceptable behavior is.*

<u>SCENARIO PREVENTION</u>: *By establishing early in their working relationship that any personal relationship was not a possibility and rejected his offer to socialize, this scenario could have been avoided.*

<u>RELATIVE TO YOU</u>: *If you want to be clearly understood, then speak directly and clearly about your feelings. If you do it with non-judgement and compassion it takes the drama out of the conversation. On first dates or meetings, its wise to have your own transportation so you are empowered to leave a situation whenever you need to.*

Although polite men of excellent character may offer to drive/carpool, if it's a new relationship, you should drive yourself until the other person has earned your trust. Good people understand this and won't try to convince you or make you feel bad about it. Plus, by letting him drive, her personal safety is in his hands. She can control how much she drinks, but not how much he drinks.

Also, it's very empowering to have enough cash to pay for your half and walk away from a situation that's become unmanageable. This is called 'no thank you' money. Never let someone who hasn't completely earned your trust buy you a drink that is made away from your direct line of site. If you can't see it the entire time, refuse it. Pay particular attention to servers and bartenders as they may have a relationship with your date and their loyalty would be to them, not you.

Neighbors - Leslie has seen Bill outside a few times. They have waved at each other but never spoke. He keeps to himself but seems friendly enough. His house is well kept, he drives a nice car, has a 9-5 job and he's married with kids.

It's a mild, sunny weekday and Leslie is cleaning the house when there's a knock at the door. She opens the door to find Bill standing there. She notices that he is clean shaven, dressed in a crisp white shirt and jeans. He says that he's home sick from work and doing a little laundry to surprise his wife, since she's always doing so much for him, but he ran out of detergent. He asks to borrow enough just for one load so he can finish and apologizes for any inconvenience.

⚑ *Her first intuition ping is that she "notices" he is clean shaven and well dressed, despite his story of being home sick. Then he shares a little too much information trying to justify his actions with a story about his wife and ends his request with an apology to deflect his request. These are manipulation tactics. Where there's a tactic, there's an agenda. Where there's an agenda, there's a red flag.*

It occurs to her that he doesn't look unwell, but it is a reasonable request and an opportunity to help out a neighbor. "Of course. I'll get it for you." She goes to fetch the detergent when he quickly follows her in. She notices he doesn't wait to be invited in, but lets it go. How could she ask a sick neighbor to wait at the door?

⚑ *A couple intuition pings here. It "occurs" to her that he doesn't look unwell and she "notices" he doesn't wait to be invited in, even though he's never been to her house before. He doesn't seem sick and the weather is perfect. Why is it necessary for him to be inside her house to wait? It is presumptuous to show up at a neighbor's asking for a favor then invite yourself in. Leslie is a helpful person so it wouldn't occur to her that these requests are anything but innocent. She didn't pick up on the initial red flags so she doesn't see that this neighbor is using laundry as an excuse to get into her house. She is already in danger.*

She directs him to the couch to wait. As soon as he walks in she has an odd thought. All of a sudden, she realizes that she is alone in the house with him. She shrugs it off and goes to get the detergent.

▷ *Her instincts turn up the volume with the feeling that she is alone with him. If his intentions were friendly, she would not perceive this aloneness in her own house. Her survival senses continue to try to show her that she shouldn't trust this "neighbor in need".*

She arrives moments later with the whole bottle to find him gone. "Bill?" No answer.

▷ *If a person you don't really know is taking liberties inside your home, like going into areas into which they haven't been invited, this is a red flag. This behavior shows a degree of disrespect or lack of regard for her space and boundaries.*

Leslie looks around and finds him around the corner in an adjoining hallway, admiring family photos. "Look at those kids. You must be a very loving mom." "Thanks." She says, a little puzzled.

▷ *Being puzzled is her intuition pinging her yet again. He is acting strange, making assumptions, wandering around her house as he pleases.*

"Here's your detergent." She tries to hand him the bottle but he asks again for just enough for one load, apologizes for the inconvenience and promises to get out of her hair.

▷ *Another apology and a promise to leave. There is no guarantee for her that he will keep his promise and he knows this. The fact that he's making a promise is a red flag. The apology is a misdirection to throw her off the scent that he is a dangerous person.*

So she goes into the kitchen to put a tupperware container together for him when she hears his footsteps behind her...

SUMMARY: *Being neighborly is part of creating a vibrant and healthy community. Dangerous criminals who blend in with their environment, like a lion in the tall grass, rely on this notion. This particular criminal was using the "neighbor in need" ruse to get permission to gain access to his target. There will be no sign of forced entry because he manipulated his way in. His story, although believable, is not very logical based on common sense. For example, any man who is home sick typically doesn't have enough energy to care about his appearance let alone to do housework. It's strange that he has enough energy to make himself presentable and do laundry but not enough energy to go to the store and buy more detergent. Even seemingly nice neighbors must be scrutinized like every other stranger before you let them into your home. Particularly if you are alone at the time they come calling.*

SCENARIO PREVENTION: *At the point where her intuition gave her enough information to question her neighbors motives, she needed to deflect all of his requests. By denying him access to her and her home, this scenario could have been avoided.*

RELATIVE TO YOU: *This is always tricky if you are new to a neighborhood or have a neighbor that's new to you. Intuition can tell you if you are in the presence of someone you need to avoid. Neighbor or not, you have the right to shoo anyone away from your house. If they need something and you're not sure about them, step outside your home to have the conversation. Tell them you're in the middle of something and you'll drop the item at their house as soon as you're done. Place the item in a bag and hang it on their front door. If you are deeply and confidently creeped out by a neighbor, call the non-emergency number of your local*

police and have an officer take a report. It might be nothing, but if it's
something, you've started a paper trail that could be very useful.

Boyfriends (or dates) - Jackie and Scott have been dating
for a few months. She's not sure if he's the one, but she really
likes this guy. He's cute, has a decent job and the sex is great.
A few things she has noticed though, Scott is a big drinker
and has gotten drunk to the point of passing out on
numerous weekends.

⊳ *Adults who need to drink to the point of drunkenness often*
have deeper issues they are running away from. Alcohol is a convenient,
legal, over-the-counter medication used to numb pain. Going unconscious
from excess use of any drug is a red flag.

Also, he's a kinda mean to waitresses and his friends are total
jerks.

⊳ *People with self-esteem issues are fond of taking advantage*
of people in the service industry. Adults who feel disempowered will take
power anywhere they can get it and food servers are low hanging fruit.
Anyone who lacks a sense of personal power to the point that they are
abusing waitresses should be avoided. Big red flag. Also, Scott has
chosen friends who aren't nice people. They are a reflection of him.

When he's around them, he turns into a complete tool. But
nobody's perfect, right? She figures it's so hard to find a cute
guy with a decent job, sometimes you just have to put up
with some stuff you don't like.

⊳ *Jackie doesn't seem overly concerned that Scott treats her*
poorly when he's with his friends. If a woman's sole criteria for
choosing a mate is based on looks and gainful employment, that can set
the stage for big problems down the road.

After a party at his friends house, he drops Jackie at her place. She's a little tweaked because he got pretty hammered and insisted, to the point of being obnoxious, that he was "fine to drive...now get in the car!"

▷ *First he disrespects her by treating her like a child and then he is incredibly reckless, taking both their lives into his inebriated hands. Her mistake is trying to avoid a scene instead of just calling a cab. She needs to let him get wound up. If he escalates to verbal or physical threats, that would be her cue to end the relationship.*

He wants to come in but she want to call it a night. It's a Thursday, she has to be up early and quite frankly, she is exhausted having just spent the last four hours tolerating the constant misogynic banter from his punk-ass friends. He says "Pleaaaase...? Just for five minutes then I'll leave. I promise" and gives her the puppy face. With a heavy sigh, she caves. She says, "Okay, but just for five minutes".

▷ *She makes it easy for him to walk all over her. When he raises his voice to intimidate or infantilizes himself (acts boyishly cute), she gives in. She hasn't given him enough push back for him to know where her boundaries are and even if she did, he may not respect them. She needs to say goodnight and not invite him in.*

He asks for a beer but she will only give him water or coffee. He doesn't want it. He plops down onto her couch, patting the cushion next to his, inviting her to sit. He's still pretty buzzed and Jackie is sober so she is not finding this cute at all. Yawning, to give him a not so subtle hint, she joins him and tells him she really has to go to bed. She doesn't want to be a bitch, but he's becoming super annoying. He promises he will leave after she gives him a good night kiss.

▷ As usual, it's all on his terms. This is a problem. He's offers a promise that she has no guarantee he will keep. How good is the word of a drunk or drugged person? He demands and she is compliant, even after she says she needs to wrap up the evening. Red flags everywhere. She needs to tell, not ask, him to leave.

The kiss turns into making out, but she has already made the mental decision to not go any further. Jackie stops, pushing gently into his chest saying softly that she needs to get up early. He interrupts her by kissing her more passionately.

▷ He shows clear signs that he is not interested in her opinion or needs in the slightest. Huge, waving red flag. He acts like the only thing that matters is what he wants, which is sex. She needs to stop the momentum, get up and open the door for him to leave.

She can tell that he's getting aroused so she pulls away and asks him to go. Undeterred, he playfully lies on top of her, saying he promises to go after a good night lay. She tries to push him off, telling him to leave.

▷ Not realizing that her boyfriend is capable of hurting her, she continues to remain passive even as she finally communicates more clearly. This direct communication came too late. Once she allows him to physically dominate her, playful or not, she dramatically reduces her opportunities to get him to leave.

In a flash, his demeanor turns from playful to angry. He puts his weight into her, pinning her down, gathering her wrists over her head, squeezing tightly and yells in her face that she is a prick tease...

SUMMARY: *The trouble began when the initial red flags (rude to waitresses and jerks for friends) went unacknowledged because they interfered with her desire to be in a relationship. It's true that* relationships require compromise but putting up with cruel or deeply intolerant behavior is different. She put his job security and bedroom performance ahead of his true character. Each time his behavior became destructive, she never gave him any feedback which led him to continue and chipped away at her self-esteem. Eventually, he escalated his bad behavior to the point where it became dangerous. This should have been an appropriate breaking point for the relationship, but she slogged on.

Getting into a car with an intoxicated person is a potentially deadly idea. The person driving is reckless and the passenger is gambling with her own life. For what? To keep the peace? Never do it. If he refuses to listen to you, promise to call the police and then do it. It's not just your lives at stake, it's also everyone else in his path.

SCENARIO PREVENTION: *After a few weeks of dating someone with a drinking problem, it's generally pretty clear that they are not a good choice as an equitable partner. As soon as she had a handful of red flags, it was time to call it quits. Removing herself from the relationship when it was clear that he had no genuine interest in her would have prevented this scenario.*

RELATIVE TO YOU: *Modern relationships are tricky. We want to share the power equally in the relationship, to have respect and feel valued. At the same time, there can be a desire for the more traditional role play. It can be confusing for both people. When troubling behaviors come up in a relationship, it's essential to address them immediately. Being able to successfully discuss "unpopular" topics is a foundation to a healthy, lasting relationship. The ability to compassionately advocate for yourself in your relationship is critical to your self-esteem. The way your message is received can tell you a lot about the character of the*

partner you've chosen. If you hit a wall but think the relationship is
worth saving, consider seeking professional counseling for both of you.

Friends of the family - Alissa is the only girl of four kids.
Mr. Bergen and his wife are good friends of her parents.
They have been friends for years. When she was a toddler,
Mr. Bergen loved to play with her. He would often pop in to
visit with her parents, with and without his wife, and Alissa
would inevitably end up in his lap. As she matured, she
would catch him staring at her. When she did, he wouldn't
break his gaze, instead he would continue and smile at her.
This made her uncomfortable but he's an adult so she shyly
looked away, hoping he would stop noticing her this way.

▷ *He was staring long enough that she would catch him so he
could let her know his interest was more than casual. It's an act of
intimidation as well. This would be considered aggressive between two
adults let alone a mature adult and pre-pubescent child. Deeply
inappropriate. Big creepy red flag.*

When she entered her pre-teen years, if ever Mr. Bergen and
Alissa were alone in the same room during parties or BBQ's,
he would never miss an opportunity to get behind her,
massage her shoulders, tell her how pretty she was and how
lucky her boyfriend must be. His touch didn't feel right but
she didn't want to make him mad by saying no. She felt like
she was in the wrong for not liking this affection.

▷ *This sort of flirtation crosses many boundaries. It's implied
consensual contact and he sexualizes the context with a reference to her
boyfriend. This is an escalation of inappropriate behavior.*

Upon leaving, he would reach his arms out and say, "Can your favorite Uncle get a hug goodbye?" If she shyly refused he would playfully charge at her, sweeping her up in his arms, to everyone's delight. This made her a little uncomfortable but she didn't want to upset her family.

▷ *Children of all ages must be allowed to define their physical boundaries. When a child refuses to hug or kiss an adult, it's natural. It's also possible the child may be acting on intuitive feedback about an adult with an agenda that other adults aren't picking up on. Not allowing or respecting the physical boundaries of a child is a red flag.*

He would write her personal notes in beautiful greeting cards, telling her about the challenges in his life and how his wife isn't a good listener. His cards included gifts, each one more expensive than the last: $10 iTunes gift card, $20 Amazon card, iPod Shuffle. He would never mail them. After a visit, they would appear in Alissa's bedroom, like magic, and always ended with instructions not to tell anyone so her brothers wouldn't find out and get jealous.

▷ *This is a dangerous escalation. Confiding in her is way beyond her maturity level and another step of developing an inappropriate relationship with her. The gifts are a trade for her silence. He is grooming her for keeping secrets and has already invaded her privacy by sneaking into her bedroom and leaving these gifts. This subtle violation speaks volumes about his arrogance, boldness and lack of conscience.*

She feels totally weird now because he makes her uncomfortable but she enjoys being showered with so much attention. He would strike up chats via email, which would sometimes include instructions to turn the ringer off on her phone so he could call her when she was in bed and not wake anyone up.

▷ *By posing as a friend who just wants to talk, it makes her more likely to give him access to her. It seems like appropriate attention and harmless in her eyes. He makes it fun and always says the right things. He has created a vice grip on her by giving her the attention that every young girl thinks she wants but doesn't know better. As the gifts become more extravagant, his behavior will become more deviant as he feels confident that her silence is bought and paid for.*

When she turned 13, he invited her to go to the mall with his wife to pick out a birthday gift. His wife had a last minute work schedule conflict so it was just Alissa and Mr. Bergen. Her parents had no reason to object to the invitation. After all, they've all known each other for years and he's practically family...

SUMMARY: *These types of scenarios are the most challenging because so much of it happens off the radar of the adults who could step in and prevent it. When Mr. Bergen began to show a special interest in Alissa, that's where the trouble began. As he escalated his inappropriate behaviors with gifts, overtures of friendship and secrets between them, she became conflicted because sometimes his attention felt creepy but other times she really liked it. He also knew that in her mind he was a safe adult. He used both of these ideas to leverage himself deeper into an inappropriate and dangerous relationship with her. He is hiding in plain sight, relying on his credibility with the family and her willingness to keep their association secret. He's extremely careful to keep the attention he gives her strategically placed so that it is invisible yet right under their noses.*

<u>SCENARIO PREVENTION</u>: *Because sexually motivated child abusers go to great efforts to mask their intentions and will spend months or years patiently grooming their targets, they can be hard to spot. Children are not necessarily likely to out their offender so it is incumbent upon parents to be vigilant. If Alissa's parents had an open dialogue with their kids about these dangers and thought to ask their daughter about Mr. Bergen early in the grooming process, this scenario could have been prevented.*

<u>RELATIVE TO YOU</u>: *It's hard to imagine that our dear friends, family and colleagues might have a dark agenda with regard to children. Because child molesters are so careful to hide their motives and actions, it's normal that a parent wouldn't think to look twice at an adult who coaches, preaches to, teaches or enjoys spending time with their child.*

Having age appropriate conversations about these types of people early and often can cultivate an environment of open communication with a child so they are likely to either come to you with strange adult behavior or talk about it if asked. Even if you don't have children, if you're aware of the red flags you might be a witness to the grooming process and an important part of prevention.

IN DETAIL: ABUSIVE RELATIONSHIPS

Husband or Boyfriend - Ella is fresh out of college and paying her dues at a menial job she doesn't like very much. After a particularly bad day, she goes to a friend's party and meets a really hot guy. After a few dates, he seems to be everything she has ever wanted. Smart, funny, charming and has a good job. She quickly falls head over heels. They have been dating for a little more than six weeks and since she spends almost every night at his place, he suggests she move in with him.

▷ *Abusive relationships often start exactly the same way, every time: A young girl who doesn't have a lot of life experience meets "the perfect guy". It moves very fast and within a few weeks or short months, he asks her to move in with him. He establishes the power dynamic by asking her to live in his place. These events generally happen together and are a red flag.*

He tells her how much he loves her, how happy she makes him and how he wants to be with her all the time. She's barely making ends meet at her lousy job and she loves him so it's perfect. Living with him is fantastic. It feels like a honeymoon.

Then, after a few weeks, Ella notices, every time she spends time with friends or family he calls and texts constantly. When she gets home, he is cold and distant which makes her feel terrible, like she's done something wrong. Ella decides that if she makes their relationship more of a priority, she can avoid that horrible cold shoulder. So she spends less time with friends/family and more time with him. This seems to make him happy. Eventually, she stops seeing her friends because it just causes too much grief.

▷ *This is a classic isolation technique used by abusers to separate their girlfriends/wives from their support system. This inhibits negative feedback and gives him more control over her. There's also an element of him completely "reliant" on her for his happiness. He makes it her responsibility and number one priority.*

He surprises Ella one day by suggesting that since he makes enough money, she should quit her crappy job. He has already said that he wants to eventually marry her and give her babies so, why not?

⊳ *This apparent act of generosity and caring is in fact a thinly veiled effort to get her to become completely dependent on him.*

Then, after a couple of months, she notices that he seems to be hanging out with his friends more and more and staying out later. When he comes home, he's drunk and not so nice. He says that she has become boring and a nag so he has to hang out with his friends to have a little fun. After all, he is the one working long hours to make sure the bills are paid. Ella takes issue, saying that she's happy to get another job and this makes him angry. Very angry. He gets in her face and yells that she has changed and is making him miserable.

⊳ *Once he has her isolated and alone with no means of income or independence, he starts the process of alienating her and chipping away at her already dwindling self-esteem.*

The next morning, Ella brings up the fight from the night before. She wants an apology but he tells her she's overreacting. He was just tired and had too much to drink and she is overly sensitive. The fights continue, when she tries to walk away, he blocks the door.

⊳ *This is another tactic to reduce her self-worth and plant the seeds of self-doubt. By diminishing his contribution to the fights and insisting that she is the one who is overly sensitive, she has less confidence about advocating for herself and starts to actually believe that she is the problem. Also, by not allowing her to leave, he is denying her any power to have an opinion or remove herself from a destructive environment. He is setting the stage to escalate the physical abuse.*

His anger grows into rage, blaming her for all of their problems. If she makes a mistake or forgets something, like picking up his beer at the store, he screams at her, calling her stupid and worthless. The fights get worse, he grabs her by the shoulders and threatens her by saying sometimes she makes him so mad, he feels like squeezing the life out of her with his bare hands.

> ▷ *Given all the dynamics that led up to the threat, it should be considered a real danger. This is 'move to an undisclosed location while he's at work and get a retraining order' level danger. He has shown himself to be abusive and given no reason to doubt that his fantasy of killing her will eventually come to fruition.*

When she tries to talk to him about these threats the next day, he acts like nothing happened, tells her that she is crazy and has a wild imagination.

> ▷ *He wants her to believe that all of his bad behavior is in her head. Once of the seeds of self-doubt have sprouted, she will question her ability to perceive things correctly and tend to believe he is right.*

One night, after a particularly rabid argument, she declares that she is going to a friend's house to stay the night. He runs into the kitchen to grab a knife then chases her into the bedroom...

SUMMARY: *This is a common scenario that unfortunately happens frequently. I spoke with Licensed Social Worker, Doris Bartel, MSW, LICSW who acquainted me with the violence wheel and the systematic approach abusers use to get into relationships and then gain power and* control. The wheel[14] represents classic behaviors that are quite consistent and reliable. The abuser sees a young, inexperienced girl as an opportunity for complete domination. That is his goal from the beginning. Being "the perfect guy" is the lure. He *declared his love for her and proved it by asking her to move in, talking about marriage and babies etc. early on. These are things that most men tend to resist and take a while to commit to, which is the first sign that he is trouble. He knows what a woman wants to hear and gives it to her. After she moved in, out of a desire to keep the peace, she allowed him to systematically dismantle her self-worth by eliminating her support system, isolating her and taking away her independence. This left her vulnerable to emotional and physical violence.

   *Another classic presentation of this dysfunctional relationship is if the woman manages to successfully leave, he may come crawling back to her on hands and knees, begging forgiveness in front of all her friends and family, pleading for her return. He will appear truly sorry, sincerely seeking her forgiveness. Everyone will buy it. Promises will be made that he will change and never do this or that again, etc. If she takes him back, his abuse will return like clockwork and the cycle will continue.

SCENARIO PREVENTION: *Being patient, taking her time and getting to know him while she remained independent could have shed light on his dark intentions thus precluding the relationship from moving forward and helping to prevent the abusive cycle.*

RELATIVE TO YOU: *It's a huge over-simplification to say we must all just choose to avoid a relationship that comes with a lot of red*

---

[14] http://www.domesticviolence.org/violence-wheel/

flags. The reality is that girls and women who already have low self-esteem or grew up with abuse tend to attract power hungry males making it extremely difficult for them to reject these men. For some women, feeling wanted or needed, even if fleeting and between abusive episodes, is a source of self-esteem.

The unfortunate reality is that power hungry men will deliver just enough of the fairy tale to keep a willing woman hanging on by a thread. Most people wouldn't put up with it, but a significant degree of personal power is needed to end a bad relationship before it becomes dangerous. Emotionally wounded women don't always have the wherewithal or self-worth to leave a bad relationship upon which they've become dependent. If you tend to attract not-so-nice men, becoming aware of the part of you that is drawn to maltreatment is the first step of healing.

SUCCESS STORIES

The following is a list of real life success stories to illustrate my point that you don't need to be as strong as a man or skilled in martial arts to successfully escape from a violent criminal. These stories highlight how acting without hesitation can save your life whether you're 3 or 53 years old. These girls and women used their instincts and willingness to defend themselves as tools for successful escape, even when confronted by criminals with guns and knives.

Read these stories through your newly educated eyes. What physical tools did they use to break the aggression equation? Which critical skills did they use to escape? Could the situation have been prevented? It's not to judge or second guess these survivors, it's to continue your mental training in awareness and keep learning. If they can do it, so can you.

> ANN ARBOR, MI - Around 11:30 p.m. on a Tuesday night, a 23-year-old woman was out for a jog. As she approached her home, a man hiding between two houses jumped out and grabbed her. He was able to hold onto her wrist and throat to control her and pushed her against a nearby tree. She was able to kick him in the groin which caused him to lose his grip. She ran home and called the police. No medical treatment was given.[15]

> LANCASTER, PA - Around 9:00 p.m. on a Monday evening, a 17-year-old female employee of Chuck E Cheese's restaurant had just gotten off work and headed toward her car in the parking lot. She was almost to her

---

[15] http://www.mlive.com/news/ann-arbor/index.ssf/2009/06/jogger_fights_off_attacker_in.html

car when someone attacked her from behind and attempted to pull her away from her car. She began to fight and he finally let her go and drove off in his car. She was not physically injured.[16]

LOS ANGELES, CA - Around 7:00 a.m. on a Friday morning, a 13-year old girl was walking to school. As she passed by a busy street, a man attacked, pushed her behind a gate and then forced her to the ground. As he attempted to sexually assault her, she was able to scream and fight with her legs, kicking him causing him to give up and flee. Despite the physical nature of the attack, the girl was uninjured. [17]

NEW YORK, NY - An 11-year-old girl was walking home from the store on a Sunday afternoon when she noticed a 19-year-old boy keeping pace with her. She knew the boy from her building, but it still made her nervous. She broke into an all out run the rest of the way home but he caught up with her in the stairwell, just shy of her apartment. He put his hand over her mouth and told her not to scream. She thought he was going to try to take her up to the roof to rape her, but instead he led her downstairs. As he forced her down the stairs, he lost a little bit of his grip on her wrist and she was able to break his grip completely. She ran outside and called for help. The neighbors surrounded and delivered some "neighborhood justice" to keep the young man from escaping until the police arrived. [18]

KINGWOOD, TX - Around 2:30 p.m. in the afternoon, a woman was walking through a pedestrian tunnel when a

16 http://lancasteronline.com/article/local/218379_Girl-fights-off-attacker-in-Manheim-Twp--parking-lot.html#ixzz25AUywhsM

17 http://www.ktla.com/news/landing/ktla-girl-fights-off-attacker,0,7758984.story

18 http://gothamist.com/2007/05/15/11yearold_fight.php

man accosted her. He held her arm and tried to force her to take off her clothes. She managed to bite him on his hand and broke his grip. She was able to run to the safety of her apartment.[19]

LONDON, ENGLAND - Around 8:30 a.m. on a Thursday, a 10-year-old girl was on her way to school. A man who had been following her eventually caught up, tried to slip a trash bag over her head and pull her off the street. He had almost gotten the bag past her ears when she kicked him in the stomach causing him to give up and run away. She was not physically injured.

SAN LUIS OBISPO, CA - Around 11:40 p.m. on a Thursday, a woman was walking through a residential area when she noticed a car drive by her very slowly then make a U-turn. A few minutes later, a man rushed up behind her and knocked her to the ground. He made a grab for her underwear as she started kicking at him. Her kicks made him back up and when he did, she was able to get up and run to a near by friend's house.[20]

PHILADELPHIA, PA - Around 4:00 p.m. a young girl and her two-year old brother were walking from the store a few blocks from their home. A man approached them from behind, picked up the little girl and attempted to take her away. She fought with kicks and bites and he dropped her to the ground. He went back after her, trying a second time to run away with her. This time, her younger brother let out a scream so loud and piercing, the attacker gave up, dropped the girl and fled.

WICHITA, KS - Around 10:55 p.m. on a Thursday, a woman drove up to an outdoor ATM. As she rolled to a

---

[19] http://abclocal.go.com/ktrk/story?section=news/local&id=8765633

[20] http://920kvec.com/pages/12784738.php?

stop, another car pulled up very close so she couldn't move her car. Then a masked man approached her side of the car with a gun pointed at her. Without hesitation, she put car into reverse and floored the gas. She managed to drive her car out of the lot and safely away. The masked gunman was found and arrested just minutes after the incident.[21]

LINCOLN, NE - Around 3:00 p.m. on a Thursday, a 17-year-old girl walked into a public restroom at a local park. A man was hiding behind a wall and when she walked in he grabbed her from behind. She was able to fight him off by using back kicks to his lower legs. Although the suspect was described as being around 6'2" tall, this teenage girl was able to break the man's grasp and escape.[22]

MADISON, WI - Around 4:00 a.m. on a Saturday, a 21-year-old woman was confronted with a man brandishing a knife. As she walked, he snuck up behind her, grabbed her, and threatened her with the knife to her neck. He forced her to follow him towards a secluded area on campus. As they were walking, he tripped over something. Taking advantage of his momentary distraction, the woman broke free and ran.[23]

CAPISTRANO BEACH, CA - On a Monday afternoon, an 8-year-old girl was returning to school from eating lunch. As she made her way along a residential street, she noticed a man who appeared to be looking at his car engine. Suddenly, he reached for the girl and tried to push

---

[21] http://www.kfdi.com/news/local/163190876.html

[22] http://www.kfor1240.com/Woman-Escapes-Would-Be-Attacker/12969894

[23] http://downtownmadison.channel3000.com/news/news/72039-woman-held-knifepoint-escapes-attacker

her into his car. She immediately began to scream, bite and kick at him until he let her go and drove off. [24]

NEW BALTIMORE, MI - Around 7:30 p.m. a 19-year-old female was delivering pizza to a motel room when a man from another room approached and started to make sexually lewd comments. She pretended like she didn't hear him. As she was walking back toward her car, the man attacked her, pulling her by the arm toward his room. She broke his grip and escaped to the safety of her car, quickly leaving the scene.[25]

SEATTLE, WA - Around 8:00 p.m. on a Sunday, a woman was walking through a residential area when a man wearing a ski mask grabbed her and threw her into his van. She was able to fight him off, get out of the van and escape. Apart from a few scratches on her hands, she was not physically hurt.[26]

---

[24] http://articles.latimes.com/1986-12-16/local/me-3405_1_capistrano-beach-girl

[25] http://newbaltimore.patch.com/articles/man-allegedly-attempts-to-assault-pizza-delivery-woman-in-chesterfield

[26] http://www.komonews.com/news/local/Officers-search-for-man-who-attempted-to-kidnap-woman-in-Greenwood-190683031.html

"Peace cannot be kept by force. It can only be achieved by understanding." - Albert Einstein

CONCLUSION

Unbreakable Woman is not *the* way to personal empowerment and safety; it is *a* way. When it comes to personal safety and empowerment, there is no such thing as being overeducated. There are so many self defense modalities (classes, DVD's, weekend workshops, books, webinars, etc.) Find what works for you. Education is important because you are important.

We have the opportunity to influence the cycle of violence from the outside-in by practicing awareness, listening to our intuition, being willing to back up verbal resistance with a commitment to physically defend ourselves all while exercising compassion for the broken, wounded personalities who act out their pain on innocent women and girls.

We can influence the cycle from the inside-out by being strong role models for our children, teaching them how to respect and value themselves and others while keeping shame, violence and humiliation out of equation. We can make a pointed effort to teach tolerance for failure and rejection. Our efforts will give younger generations coping devices that will get them through life without the need to bully or dominate someone to feel better about themselves.

Compassion is a tool to help bring "monsters" into the light of humanity. Understanding what you have in common with these people will do more to help you stay safe and empowered than learning to fight out of fear. Empathy shines a bright light on these men, illuminating their vulnerabilities and highlighting your strengths.

By understanding the turbulent childhoods that create violent criminals and how many types of personalities can sprout from those influences, you can accept the cold, hard truth that any stranger is capable of anything. Strangers cannot surprise you if you are educated about their tactics and consistently practice awareness.

By cultivating the critical skills you were born with, you can remain centered, confident and off the radar of those looking for easy targets.

This book is designed to be your companion. To reinforce your strengths and the incredible things you already know how to do. To help you practice mental training so you have a space in your brain for every possibility and a habit of seeing yourself successfully escaping any dangerous situation. This will keep you out of denial and in the moment, where you are the most powerful.

My ultimate goal is to help you experience the paradigm shift from fear to confidence through education. Read and re-read the pages that resonate the most with you. Repetition is the mother of learning.

If we accomplished our mission together, this book didn't transform you into an Unbreakable Woman... It reminded you that you already are.

SECTION VI

Bibliography

Bartel, Doris MSW, LICSW. Personal Interview (January 11, 2012)

Caignon, Denise, Groves, Gail. Her Wits About Her (First Edition). New York: Harper & Row, 1987

Centers For Disease Control and Prevention: Black, M.C., Basile, K.C., Breiding, M.J., Smith, S.G., Walters, M.L., Merrick, M.T., Chen, J., & Stevens, M.R. (2011). The National Intimate Partner and Sexual Violence Survey (NISVS): 2010 Summary Report. Atlanta, GA: National Center for Injury Prevention and Control, Centers for Disease Control and Prevention, http://www.cdc.gov/

De Becker, Gavin. The Gift of Fear Survival Signals That Protect Us From Violence (First Edition). New York: Little, Brown & Company, 1997

Frankel, Lois P. Women, Anger & Depression Strategies For Self-Empowerment. Deerfield Beach: Health Communications, Inc., 1992

Hazelwood, Robert, R., Burgess, Ann W. Practical Aspects of Rape Investigation A Multidisciplinary Approach (Third Edition). Boca Raton: CRC Press, 2001

Holmes, Stephen T., Holmes Ronald M. Profiling Violent Crimes An Investigative Tool (Second Edition). Thousand Oaks: Sage Publications, Inc., 1996

Rape Abuse & Incest National Network: National Institute of Justice & Centers for Disease Control & Prevention. Prevalence, Incidence and Consequences of Violence Against Women Survey. 1998; U.S. Department of Justice. 2003 National Crime Victimization Survey. 2003; U.S. Bureau of Justice Statistics, Sex Offenses and Offenders. 1997; 1998 Commonwealth Fund Survey of the Health of Adolescent Girls. 1998; U.S. Department of Health & Human Services, Administration for Children and Families. 1995 Child Maltreatment Survey. 1995; U.S. Bureau of Justice Statistics. 2000 Sexual Assault of Young Children as Reported to Law Enforcement. 2000; World Health Organization. 2002; U.S. Department of Justice. 2005 National Crime Victimization *Survey. 2005. Rape Abuse & Incest National Network Statistics. Retrieved 2011 from http:// www.rainn.org/statistics*

Made in the USA
Charleston, SC
02 May 2013